7 DAYS TO
TRANSFORM YOUR
LIFE

Cathi Hargaden

Contents

Thank You to

Kathleen Blong & Michael Joseph Hargaden

For their Creativity & Eccentricity

PREFACE

What is around you is within you! The physical world is nothing but the manifestation of the invisible world and our inside worlds. So what is around you is repeat messages of what defines who you are. If you are surrounded by chaos, clutter then that is going to affect how you feel about yourself and who you think you are. All these cues and clues are around us in our homes, workspaces, broadcasting messages and reflecting back our identities.

I was first introduced to Feng Shui when I invited a friend to my apartment. She looked around and commented on it having naturally good Feng Shui. I asked what that meant. I took to the concept immediately. I understood the whole idea of energy vibrating through colour, design, sound, aroma and alchemy instantly.

I was taught by architects the wisdom and function of this ancient philosophy. It took me all over the world being fascinated by cultural geographical and political geometry with a flow of history and rich messages for all to hear. I was struck with great intrigue and curiosity by all aspects of Feng Shui and once acquainted with the ideas I began to teach and learn even more.

7 Days To Transform Your Life

When I started to study Feng Shui, I reflected upon the environments of my own childhood and life.

My earliest memories are of playing in a derelict building wondering how I could improve it. Prefabricated buildings designed for the short-term after the war years were now on the verge of being pulled down.

Street after street after street was being pulled down on the way to school in a concrete city. No flowers, plants or trees were evident. Most colours were grey and brick and the only reprieve was a very small garden my mother cultivated lifting the whole street to the Gardens of Babylon.

Growing up in the 1960's not everybody owned a car in the U.K. so people often stayed in the same environment. There was nothing to compare different places to where you lived. But in my case, our family went off to Ireland every year for a month. An unheard of feature in our neighbourhood but it was the annual journey to what I perceived as Nirvana.

I became aware how some places made me feel great, expansive and free whilst others were constricted, limiting and dour. I found that some environments gave me a more expansive perception of life whilst others seemed limiting and restrictive.

The impoverished inner city school limited any educational development, restricted our repertoire as individuals and severely cut down any aspirations one could possibly have had for one's future.

Until, five of us got a golden opportunity to attend two more years of education in a suburban convent higher school.

The differences in environment mesmerised me. I was stunned by the beauty of the space in which these students were so privileged to study — trees galore, boundless fields, and pink plum blossom trees with petals falling like confetti. Those students who were used to it did not seem to notice and were surprised by my response.

The street I grew up on was my world. The environment in which I lived defined my first business. The famous football clubs of Liverpool and Everton were situated close by. Fans came in droves, parking their cars in our street. This only meant one thing! Business! The Business was looking after the cars of the devoted fans whilst they watched their heroes at the football match.

I minded their cars whilst at the match, and then turned up for payment when the game was over.

Next Business? A wasteland. Literally a piece of wasteland next to a very popular street market. This market had been very famous during the years of trade at Liverpool's dock. We resorted to the wasteland next to it where no fee was required and we could set up and sell our wares. At the time of doing this I recall studying T. S. Eliot's "The Wasteland". Out of the worst environment a wasteland, we created a business!

Environments shape all of us, good, bad and indifferent. I went on to live in Greece, California, Canada, and India – great experiences for realising how environments define our identities. Travelling throughout the Far East, Middle East, North and Central America, Europe, India I realised that how environments are set up affects internal aspirations and often defines limitations and self-esteem.

I have worked with clients in the U.K. for health, medical and social reasons. People from all backgrounds know or are aware of this invisible space, energy and feeling. I have done Feng Shui consultations for diverse cultural and religious backgrounds. It appeared people had issues with their spaces all over the world! Environments and the places people live in are defined by what people are thinking and feeling within them. From clutter, to bad neighbours, to sick building syndrome and acrimonious break ups the list is endless.

People know that something within the home has to CHANGE!

My experiences with Feng Shui taught me about what to look for when buying and renting properties. One of the houses I was selling had been designed with a beautiful balance using the Feng Shui principles and the 5 energies of nature. I had two prospective buyers. Both of them wanted the house within ten minutes of being in the home. Why? It made them FEEL a certain way. One guy said he wanted to buy it just because of one picture on the wall! Yes people make decisions about big things in their lives on an emotional basis all the time. I know I have. Even though he was buying a huge house it was the picture that influenced his decision!

It has been the same for attracting tenants. Setting up the house to attract the right calibre of person with respect and integrity for their space is essential to landlords. As soon as people walked in they wanted to rent the property instantly. Of course location played a part, but it's how the space makes people feel that matters the most. That feeling has been set up so people feel good, relaxed, harmonious and balanced within themselves. From colour, to orientation, aroma and symbolism people are allured by a feeling, which was created using the Feng Shui principles.

At the many institutions I taught the subject of decluttering, space clearing and Feng Shui the students repeatedly returned to the classroom telling me what had shifted in their lives. Here is just some of the feedback:

- Better night's sleep
- "Removing her clutter her dreams arose out of the clearance."
- Got rid of the spouse once and for all to start a new chapter
- One student met someone and got married as a result
- People reported better clarity of thinking

- More business clients resulted
- More money flowing in the form of gold and silver
- Expansion from one bedroom property into a penthouse suite
- Attracting more clients on **Airbnb** than they required

This book has been talking to me for many years. It is not just about transformation through Feng Shui but about all the other subsidiary subjects I have discovered and experienced. I discovered the power and the vibration of sounds, aromas, spiritual philosophies, symbolism, designs, geometry, mathematics of spaces, and archetypes upon our spaces and places. The book has been borne out of entering so many homes as an occupational therapist and realising if people had control over their own space they would feel more at peace and healthier.

It also comes from a background of visiting and living in other countries where their attitude to space and energy is very different. In some societies it is essential to cleanse the home, protect it and have a get together to celebrate the new space. In Canada, I won a research award for community radio. I visited some of the reservations where the people see themselves as the guardians of Mother Earth, they own nothing and their view of life is cyclical and integrated with the five elements of Nature. This in turn affected the space in which they lived. I lived in Crete, Greece, where the ancient tradition of protection using the evil eye was an everyday essential.

Coming from an Irish background the folklore, symbolism and designs of the Celtic culture is punctured by how our spaces, buildings are arranged to affect our feelings on the inside. The interest in Feng Shui took me to the amazing Islamic features found throughout the world with their famous geometric and labyrinthine designs. Throughout my travels to Morocco, Tunisia, Egypt, Jordan, Oman, UAE, Kashmir, India, Zanzibar you can see how the designs of homes, spaces have an internal effect upon the sensibilities and spirit. You walk through arches, the eye follows the designs and already you begin to feel good in the space around you.

In Broome, Australia I saw the amazing Feng Shui Chinese Designs littered along the coast where the Chinese pearl divers operated. In the Islands of Fiji, Bali, Cook Islands you see the large faces of people designed to frighten off un-welcome visitors to their homes and space. Protection of one's space has always been fundamental to human survival.

The world is littered with places that hold an energy of desecration, sadness and huge human emotional dislocation: the convicts of Van Dimien's Land (Tasmania) and the remains of their prisons; the dungeons of East Africa in Tanzania still marking the fate of the slaves imprisoned there. A church is now built on the site of the old slave market. Sometimes I wonder if other structures are built to eradicate the pain and sorrow of what has gone before. No design or building can ever wipe out the patterns of misery experienced by millions.

7 Days To Transform Your Life

There are houses where people were terrorized and children were murdered. This is more of an extreme version of why people repel certain places for living purposes. They know they can feel the negative energy in such places.

So the spaces and places in which we live, work and socialise all have a specific energy created by the mind. Everything on the outside of us has come from someone's mind. That is why setting up your own environment with the messages, cues and directions you want to resonate with is very important for your health, wealth and relationships.

This book is about preparing yourself for the specific transformation you would like to attract. It is like preparing the table to sit at and eat. With preparation comes expectation and creativity. Of course you have to go and make the meal. You are preparing your surroundings for the kind of feelings, vibration and energy, which serve up a menu that you would like to, orient yourself towards in your life. Your space at home serves up cues, on a daily basis it reflects back the messages you have set up for yourself. Cluttered surroundings serve up self-sabotage and procrastination. Repeated messages serve up the same repeated results. Repetition is one of the ways marketers sell us food, clothes, dreams and lifestyles. That is why setting up repeated messages of the reality you want to relate to is essential. Your environment invites you to interact with it unlike the passive dormancy of the TV monitor. If you want transformation, you have to activate the messages, the opportunities that you have designed around you. You are the architect of your own life. You have to be ready to meet the opportunities half way.

The expression "If only walls could talk" rings true when every place has a story to tell and it shows up in the very fibres of the home. It does not go away. It hangs in the air for years, for centuries. You can dissipate those webs of energy and create your own better vibrant webs by joining me in this journey in the next Seven Days!

Put simply it is now an opportunity to focus on your own space by creating for yourself a vision of your life within the inner sanctum of your own home or business. **It is time to set up your secret code within your own walls so you can orient your life choices; setting sail in the direction you wish to go.**

INTRODUCTION

The phrase 'you are what you eat' refers to the fact that your wellbeing and health is directly linked to what you eat and drink.

Garbage in and garbage out is an expression regarding what you feed your mind. You decide what you think about.

And, so it is that what is around you is within you. Your personal space/environment is reflected back to remind you how you are on the outside is how you are on the inside. That every thought, decision, choice, idea is laid out all before you to reflect and communicate back to you – this is Your Life. This is Your Story. You decide where your path leads and how the journey feels.

Nikola Tesla once said,

"If you wish to understand the universe, think of energy, frequency and vibration".

How does your energy, frequency and vibration affect your space?

It is these qualities that influence how you feel when you enter a space of any kind. Whether it's a house, shop, hospital or a religious, corporate or political building. It is the difference between attraction and repulsion. For example which would you be attracted to, a rubbish dump or a beautiful garden? Both these landscapes hold different energies, frequencies and vibrations. Compare the foul smells of burnt waste to the feelings evoked by flowers and green growth. Usually people want to feel elevated, inspired, rejuvenated and expansive. Environments that create this feeling are awe-inspiring. Architects, builders, and masons spent centuries designing and building places that allowed people to feel peaceful and healed.

As Churchill once said,

"We shape our buildings and then thereafter they shape us".

However, there are many spaces in the world that pull your own inner energy downward. Where atrocities have occurred people often comment that no birds are ever found singing or nobody wants to live there again. It often leaves behind a "feeling" of tragedy, of loss and sadness with a deafening silence.

It is no different when you go into your own home, business or retail space. Where there has been conflict and arguments amongst people, the feeling often lingers in the air. Anyone coming into that space can sense a feeling of resistance.

Have you ever noticed that when you walk into some places to rent or buy you instantly know this is it? Yet, when you enter other rentals or houses they repel you and intuitively you know that this is not the place for me.

Spaces that don't feel great can sometimes be painted white almost to negate those unwanted feelings. However, energetic patterns of defeat, negativity, and trauma still prevail because there is no attempt to deal with the invisible spider webs of energy left behind. Abraham Lincoln once said **"To believe in the unseen is a triumph and a blessing as the rational mind is always a faithful servant."** First Nation American Indians knew all about this world of the unseen and would never settle in a plot of land without cleansing it first. This was a demonstration of their reverence for Mother Earth and an awareness of unseen energetic forces.

The principles of FENG SHUI:

WIND   **WATER**

风   **水**

FENG   **SHUI**

These two Chinese symbols mean Wind and Water. They are two elements from nature that appear non-tangible or not that important but in actual fact they shape everything around us. The mountains, forests, trees are all sculpted by these two forces that adapt and flow.

It is no different in our own lives. We are mostly made up of water and the wind/energy that blows through our lives shapes our experiences and life.

Water holds memory—like a geometry and at the most cellular level of our bodies there are memories about our ancestry, our origins and the nature of our cells; known as DNA.

The inner geometry and composition of who we are at a cellular level is vibrating with what is around us all the time. Dr Bruce Lipton in his lecture on Biology of Belief, is saying that the formation of our cells resonates with the environment and what is in that environment is resonating back to our cells influencing our perceptions of our reality. So if there are toxins in the environment such as; high levels of moisture or pollutants and poisons, shapes of buildings, smart meters, aromas, sounds—they all influence how we resonate, feel and perceive our reality.

Historically people have used smell if an odour was foul indicating danger. We have used sounds to determine if there was a friend or foe i.e. bells, trumpets, and horns. Colours indicated trouble or harmony; green for nature and red for Danger.

Feng Shui is about harnessing the best energies to live in. Buildings and spaces have been designed in such a way as to create harmony and proportion. Feng Shui has been a secret code of complex mathematic compass precisions, astrology and the basic tenets of The Book of Changes in Taoism.

The philosophy of Taoism honours the flow and changing landscape of the natural world. It recognizes the world of the divine that connects everything in creation. But human perception of reality identifies with a world of polarities. Good versus bad. Right and wrong, Up and down. The Book of Changes known as the 'I Ching' explains how everything is always in a constant state of flux. It illustrates how we constantly fluctuate between two extremes in our journey in Life; those extremes are the states of yin and yang. They represent the opposite energies of life and the place of peace is neutrality and balance. This is the place when you feel you can let go with no decision or conflict and just be at peace with yourself. There is always the opposite and the complementary two sides to everything. The principles of yin and yang demonstrate that opposite's conflict and complement every situation, be it externally in the world or internally within our own minds and hearts. In our own lives we constantly hover between the two extremes. One day we might be very depressed the next day elated for no reason at all. In understanding the principles of yin and yang; you cannot have one without the other. In the Tao Te Ching :

"Under heaven all can see beauty as beauty only because there is ugliness.

All can know good as good only because there is evil.

Therefore having and not having arise together.

Difficult and easy complement each other.

Long and short contrast each other.

Voice and sound harmonize each other,

Front and back follow one another."

Lao Tzu

The Book is basically saying that the only **permanence in life is change or transformation** and that through any one lifetime humans can experience sixty-four different situations from the darkest moments to the most successful and fulfilling. Then, of course, there is everything in between.

Access to Feng Shui information was extremely limited and secretive. It was primarily the monks who knew how to layout buildings in such a way that the Emperor had control over the masses through controlling the environment.

The Ruling Emperor of China would prefer no change in order to stay in power. One way of asserting great control over their subjects was to define the environment so that what the people saw around them all the time told them one message; the Emperor Rules!

Has anything really changed? In our world today we have marketing and advertising messages surrounding our environments reminding us of the most important people who hold power that include: corporations, banks, the politicians, the celebrities, old monarchies, historical families of great wealth, with the rest of the people holding very little power.

The common symbol of Taoism is yin and yang.

Yang has the characteristic qualities we associate with as an outgoing forceful energy; strong, aggressive, power and "go get it" energy. We can have yang colours of bright red, orange or yin colours of pale blue and green. It is with these two types of energies that we interpret our life, our foods and of course our environment.

Yin is gentler, yielding, and bends. It is flexible and there are great qualities to this. We cannot know of yang qualities until we experience yin qualities.

Both forces have positive and negative charges. And so it is the same for the space we live in. Some spaces are very yang; that is they are very loud, bright spaces required for their function. e.g. children's' playgrounds, corporate design, retail or entertainment spaces. Then there are those that are quiet and peaceful—such as hospitals, healing centres, and hospices.

The aim is to create good health and wealth and stable relationships by balancing the environment. How we manage these two forces can have a massive impact on our lives. If we find ourselves heading towards an extreme YANG lifestyle and yang surroundings that would be a life out of control for whatever reasons be it, addictions, reactions to situations, responses that are aggressive. A YIN life may be one of total retreat, no voice, no stance. This book will help you understand these two forces and how to make them work for you.

The energy that is around us is coming from within us. That is why what you see on the outside that is, your own environment or home YOU created it from the inside. Symbols of water and wind are important messages because they remind us that everything needs to flow. It is only when we run into obstacles be they physical, mental or emotional that they start to create a feeling of ill at ease or disease itself. We can relate this to the body. If we don't have enough oxygen in circulation for instance when there is a clot in the body then it may stop the functioning of the whole system. This then results in an embolism, stroke, varicose veins, or amputation due to the tiny capillaries not receiving sufficient oxygen. The blood, the lymphatic system and oxygen have to flow otherwise areas of the body become dead. Like the space in the home, or parts of our life, if we do not give it energy or oxygen, they wither and die over time.

This applies to our own spaces where we work and live. If there is nothing to relate to in the space, what is there to flow with? If there is too much stuff in your space then you may become psychologically, physically, emotionally blocked. It can take place over years, The accumulation piles up and you wake up to find that you have buried yourself with nowhere to move. The distractions around you become weapons of procrastination, self sabotage and unfocused thinking.

In between those two opposites of energy – yin and yang – which are found within each other, are finer attuned energies that are around us daily in our spaces. They are the representation of the five elements or five different energies.

7 Days To Transform Your Life

The Five Elements are pivotal to understanding the philosophy behind Feng Shui as they represent the five kinds of energy essential for health, wealth and balance, found throughout our world. They are earth energies, water, fire, wood and metal.

What do these five energies have to do with your home, business or any space?

When you have a balance of each of these five energies represented symbolically or physically they create the magic feelings for people, feeling elevated, grounded, flowing, supported and creative. The elements are used in a way that create that secret ingredient. The kind of feeling that when you walk into a place it is talking to YOU, inviting YOU to stay there longer because it stimulates the eyes, the aroma creates a sensation that pleases, the sounds are enough to know that all your internal cues are easing their way into this space of empowerment for you! With this secret knowledge you create your own alchemy of balance, success and freedom.

It is almost like your inner mind is resonating with your surroundings—your space is the product of the seeds you planted. What are the messages you choose to surround yourself – what ideas, scenes, feelings have you created around you that come to fruition in your life? Your space whether it is retail, or home, is like a garden. What you put in there starts to create a relationship with the people living there. It does not take long for people to become aligned with what is around them twenty-four hours a day. You may ask yourself what was the picture of childhood that affected you? The colours of the walls, the aroma that pervaded the house, the plants, the ornaments or the wallpaper. Repetition is what sells us an idea, a product or an experience. What we see each and every day is communicating a message; does it feel good? Great, if not then change it.

What I realised is that the only power people really ever have in their lives is what is around and within the space they reside in. Once you step out of the door you are exposed to many things you have no control over. However, having control of what is influencing you within your own four walls comes down to being awake and aware.

What This Book will Cover:

Transformation what is it? It is changing or making a marked change in form, nature, or appearance, a process by which one figure, expression, or function **is** converted into another. The kind of transformation that makes a change from something that no longer works for you to something better for You.

Sometimes it is our habits that keep us where we are in a fixed state. When there is no flow or movement naturally taking us forward, change is usually forced upon people through a trauma or circumstances, which in turn places people into a new space or a new reality. For example, divorce, a death, fire, murder, a financial loss. We become stuck because we are often blinded by our habits. Our habits support our comfort zone and there is nothing wrong with comfort. Having a flow in life does require change and so it is knowing what needs to change and when.

This book is an invitation to transform your life in ways that shift your space inside—that is what you feel and think—to what you focus on in and around you daily. It is an opportunity to instigate those changes from yourself by taking action and control of your own environment rather than waiting for some outside force to instigate it. These changes are not dependent upon anybody other than YOU although they will affect the other people you reside with.

Even if you have other people to contend with, clearing clutter and making those changes within that space can be beneficial to others. You may even get some thanks!

How is this going to be possible?

If you really want transformation in your life, and are prepared to take action then this is the book for you.

The alternative?

Staying with the existing painful patterns that torture people daily with chaos, mental fog, confusion, and no focus on what would please them. Do people want to choose more sameness? Do they want to become passive victims of piped through news media, politicians? Are they happy to settle with low level energetic entertainment that keeps them in the same place at all times? When people are confined to the same space over and over with no change, they are doomed to reflect the same life patterns over and over again.

I have witnessed people putting up resistance even to the point of illness and disease rather than change their minds and life. And the irony is that change can come one minute at a time. It doesn't have to be a revolutionary change.

So, this book is about preparing yourself for wealth, health and relationships and that starts with what is around you. This book will give you the tools, steps to start laying the foundations of what it is you want to become and experience in your life. If you don't prepare the table to eat then nothing shows up. The same with your life; if you don't make the preparations by starting with cues and symbols in and around your space how can you expect what it is you want to show up? You have to create the foundation, the images the feelings around you first. This book will take you day-by-day on how to shift those changes slowly but surely.

I want to at this point emphasize you do not have to live in the "right" area or "right location" to implement these seven days of transformation. I come from what was deemed a very deprived area but because of certain influences we made the environment creative on next to nothing. I used those influences to springboard me to other horizons. I do know that environments can limit you in terms of connections, people who perceive differently, and the elements around you have a softening or hardening effect. The scenery and influences around you are talking all the time – ask yourself what are they saying?

You have to script your story no matter where you live. Do not fight for your limitations within the parameters of the environment in which you find yourself living. Go beyond those confines, and create something bigger, greater and expansive

I also want to emphasize that accepting wherever you are or whatever you are doing now is imperative. What you resist persists. Acceptance is always a great catalyst for change. I realize I spent too much energy and time on resisting. I was in a career, which I resisted, and not wanting to be there most of the time. One day I realized just how much what I was doing had immense value to peoples' lives. I was changing people's lives and I had a huge responsibility in the process. It was a feeling of accepting exactly where I was now. In doing so, I let go of struggle. Within two weeks of that feeling I was gone from the job, the career and entered a creative zone. I had acknowledged the value of what I was doing and with that came an acceptance. So, let go into where you are now and keep the messages around you positive, holistic and aspirational.

Don't forget to contact me when you realize the enormity of the results you receive.

Day 1

Without doubt, within the first day of moving OUT your clutter, changes will start to appear. Many people end up clearing out their desks or throwing out bags of clothes whilst listening to my webinars. By the end of the webinar they feel better!

Day 2

You start to clear the invisible clutter- that which stands and creates a dank, sad, untoward, restrictive feeling but you cannot see or touch it. Using some ancient and simple cost effective techniques you can be certain the house will begin to rock.

Day 3

We are going to shift all movement and focus on the inner architecture as you realize **everything within you is outside of you!** This day is a must because without daring to see what is inside of you how can you ever know what reality you wish to attract?

Day 4

You are introduced to the five elements earth, water, metal, fire and wood. You will perceive your environment through a pair of new eyes so you can create that balance you desire.

Day 5

This is all about creating your very own Feng Shui Vision Board. This board assists you in understanding that the flow and cycles in your life have a pattern or a code. This is an opportunity to make your visions part of the pattern you want in your life.

Day 6

Using the secret code of Feng Shui we imprint the visions and dreams from yesterday in and around our spaces reflecting back to us all the time this is how I want to be, how I want to feel, and where I am going.

Finally, Day 7

Power hubs in our own homes enable us to harness the energies of those areas for the maximum progress and development in our life. There have been places and spaces designed right across the world to attract the highest energy and powers in order to control others. As a royal family member recently announced, "Palaces are designed to intimidate".

Once you have made shifts in these three power areas you start to feel and live the difference for you and your family. Of course, let us not forget about the inhabitants. **You** are the person holding all the energy with the capacity to make the frequencies, vibrations and resonances the best for your home, business or commercial space.

DAY 1 – CLUTTER

Awareness of the space you find yourself in allows you to look at it from afar and ask what effect is it having on you and anyone living on the premises.

Have you ever found yourself not being able to think clearly because there is too much going around you and in your head? Whatever is inside of you is reflected on the outside and vice-versa.

Is This You?

The clutter of your environment can stop you from moving and flowing easily through your home, work or any space. Obstructions that are obvious (like a bag or shoes in the way) can cause accidents. But sometimes these obstructions in our homes and lives are not always that obvious. They can be far more subtle, to the point that we are not aware that they exist.

Sometimes using the analogy of acupuncture helps to illustrate the principles of energy being able to flow freely in and around your home. Like the blood and lymphatic system circulating around our body, it is important to keep the arteries and veins clear from any obstructions. If we have too much surrounding us in environments it is almost impossible to breathe, move freely, and adapt. We become restricted, rigid and ultimately frozen physically, mentally and emotionally.

Acupuncture is designed, by the use of needles, to release blockages internally and allow the natural flow of the chi to move around as normal. It is similar to the removal of blockages within your home of clutter, hoarded materials blocking your rooms, cellars and passages. These are items no longer functional or of any great value and yet you hang on, you hang on, you hang on...Yes, this is the problem. It is so hard to let go within and without.

There is a list in the index of what can be considered to be **clutter** but only you know what clutter is to you. I am not suggesting getting rid of sentimental items but you may wish to consider that the more you hold onto things of the past the less room there is for a future with space. We all have clutter and we are unable to dispense with it overnight. Clearing your clutter is a process. It is a cycle like the five elements with a beginning, middle and an end.

It is not necessarily just about being neat. People who do not have any obvious disarray on the outside can often disguise their erratic behavior/way of thinking by throwing things into cupboards or stuffing things into drawers. Control comes in many different ways.

As an occupational therapist and Feng Shui Consultant I have entered over 2000 homes throughout the UK, and Australia, Ireland and India and I can tell you that people have stuffed into their homes so much that their clarity of thinking is impaired, creativity is blocked and in some cases people physically could not move from one room to the next with any ease. The nature of the work I did allowed me access to every room of the home so I saw the insides of people's lives. Some of my clients have wondered why they are unable to keep any of the money they have earned, or why nobody new has come into their space and then they look around and see the reactions of where they live.

Here are some examples:

In Ireland one guy had been left a huge rectory home where every room was crammed to the brim of all his mother's belongings. He reached such depths of despair, as he just did not know where to begin. So, sorting out which room is the first point to start and then how to proceed was the priority. I have to say we had huge bouts of laughter with the Irish music in the background for effect and whilst this was an extreme case sometimes just taking the first step is all people require.

I visited one client who had a very sick child who had no energy to mobilise around the home. When I entered the living room it was jammed full of boxes and the parents explained they were about to decorate. They were also running a health business, which is why the boxes were choking up the whole downstairs. I did suggest clearing away the clutter but when I returned much later on they were in the same situation. What is around you affects how you feel, think and what you do. Often it is difficult for people to see the correlation between their health and their environment. We all fail at times to see what is right in front of us.

What about the man in the wheelchair who surrounded himself with his lifetime collector's magazines, trains sets, and other memorabilia. He could no longer mobilize in the wheelchair because there was no space left to do so. It was almost as though he had made himself a hostage to his own environment. His quality of life had totally diminished with absolutely nowhere to move to.

One man had placed all his rubbish in the kitchen 20 plastic bags and this caused him some emotional upset. Another lady would not let me into the house initially because she felt shame and guilt for the environment she was living in. It was a reflection back to her mental state of feeling depressed, low and could not see a way out of it.

What about the elderly couple in there eighties? I turned up to visit them and they were sitting outside in deck chairs – they seemed to be having a great time basking in the sun. However, when I went inside they both confessed that the reason why they were sitting outside was because there was nowhere for them to sit inside- they had acquired clutter over sixty years and told me they had no intention of sorting it.

In one particular office a woman approached me and asked if I knew of any way she could make extra money as her job was not paying her enough. I asked her what her home looked like. She told me it was totally cluttered and felt she couldn't do anything with it. I said go back and clear it. Some months later I asked how did it go- reportedly the place was still the same.

As T. Harv Eker says,

"How you do anything is how you do everything".

The list is endless of peoples' lives being thwarted either for health, wealth or relationship reasons predominantly due to the energetic fog they surround themselves in. Clutter is often very uncomfortable and a source of great embarrassment to many; it's as though people will look into their very heart and view the disturbances, conflicts, sadness and memories all in one go.

Above all, what really trips people up metaphorically is the degree of procrastination in their lives. The environment supports this constant hesitancy and delay because to look around and see chaos disrupts any flow whether in movement or an idea. Clutter distracts focus and then we realize time has ticked on and we are in the same place with the same set of clutter.

WHY DO YOU HAVE CLUTTER AND WHAT IS IT DOING

Clutter robs your time. Think of all the obstacles you have to negotiate when the home, workspace or business is not clear and simple. Time is money – it's the ultimate commodity, the asset that no one can buy back. The more you find yourself in a cluttered environment it actually consumes more time and effort in getting anything accomplished. Having this clutter around you is costing you money because you carry with you the vibrations it creates. Clarity is wealth because when you go straight to the point of what you need to do effectiveness brings more positive results.

To make any kind of change requires effort, energy to do so. If you can clear your clutter you can take on new ideas, learn a new skill and much more. But if you cannot make the connection that having a permanent clutter energy around you fogs what else you do then how can you change? So, lack of money was still going to be an issue for the lady in the office – if a person couldn't do the basics, clear her clutter how is he/she going to deal with managing money? Clearing the clutter would give anyone the clarity to take the next step for a new job. So the clutter created a self-fulfilling prophecy of being stuck, being stuck in the stuckness until the stuckness becomes an identity.

STEP ONE

WHAT CLUTTER IS: Clutter is anything physical that is around in your environment and no longer has a function, holds energies that are not supportive of who you are today, creates distress if looked at, excess matter that serves no purpose, storage of goods in case one day you might use them. In fact, the best way of describing clutter is weapons of mass distraction. It distracts people from a focus in their lives, from clarity in ideas and in a business it is the ultimate blockage.

WHY YOU HAVE CLUTTER: There are many reasons. One is the generational difference. Those brought up during Second World War find it difficult to throw things away as they were brought up with a scarcity mentality. The younger generations accumulate products, throw them to one side and acquire an update. People are surrounded in a soup of clutter and it is a manifestation of what is going on within their psychological state. These things start to encroach on what is an already smaller amount of living space for many people across the world.

Architecture of inner cities has bundled people into smaller and smaller living spaces so the ability to move freely is far less when you keep acquiring more and more. Not forgetting that we have been programmed to be a consumer population, which results in an accumulation of more stuff

WHAT IS IT DOING TO YOUR LIFE: It affects people.

Health –The chaos may cause mental instability as well as tripping over stuff. I once lived in a house with a family where the first room from the entrance was where everything was just thrown in and I mean EVERYTHING!

When I went into that room to iron I felt chaotic, disturbed almost, and I could see this manifesting in the personalities of the household.

There are psychological reasons in terms of safety, support, a feeling of not having enough, comfort and control as to why people set this environment up like that. At the same time people can often feel trapped by what is around them and not know how to escape it.

Wealth – if you are creating a business from home or studying for a career you have to have clarity and discipline – these two qualities enable people to go forward with their ideas and execute them. If there are too many distractions because of the environment the energy becomes cluttered, ideas are dissipated easily and the thinking confused. Now there are even more weapons of distraction from phone devices, to TV's, monitors everywhere often in every room in the home. Where is there a space to get away from anything that is competing for your attention?

Relationships – Two people living together in close confines have to compromise in how they choose to live in that space. One person overriding another's space epitomizes the relationship and the amount of freedom each accords the other.

STEP TWO - PREPARATION

Before throwing out everything or anything and creating even more chaos be alert to pre-planning. How do you intend to start?

I teach people to draw out a plan of their space; whether it is home, business or workplace. Once drawn, they need to colour the areas that need the most attention. Often it can be the entrance, the functional rooms of bathroom and kitchen. Prioritize what is the first, second and so on.

Before initiating this process there is a mental, emotional and functional preparation and dimension to a task like clearing away visible and invisible obstructions. Sometimes the clutter is there to disguise other fears in one's life. When you take out many items you are left with just space. How then does that space define you if everything you owned felt like part of your identity? When some space is finally created, people's health and mental clarity often improve and they can breathe much deeper as though it is a release. Be aware that in such a process as this there comes a healing crisis – that is a feeling of strangeness and not feeling quite right but eventually you grow into the new space.

- Draw the area;
- Prioritize which area is the most important and don't forget that this is a process. See Clutter List in the Index.
- Identify what you no longer need. That includes mementoes, and anything non-functional or is of no use to you anymore.
- One day you will be forced to let go of everything so it may as well be with your blessing that it is let go of in the way you want as opposed to someone dashing it away in a skip! That is why it is best to take the time to intermittently deal with what you own and put it to a good resource. If you do not have any love for it then let it go.

How do I know? Because I have seen it happen hundreds of times ... no one cares about your mementoes, photos will be binned and the precious items resold back into the earth's energy.

STEP THREE – MAKE A DATE

Clearing away matter is by no means just a physical activity. It requires a mental and emotional awareness because decisions have to be made about the minor details to the bigger obstructions in the space.

Making excruciatingly painful or simple decisions requires energy no matter its importance. So, mentally gearing yourself up for the task is essential.

- Pinpoint a date and time to start
- Do you need others to help or is it a lone sojourn?
- Energy is everything so ensuring you have psychological apparatus to get started is important too.
- Eat properly before starting, as what you eat and how you feel determines decisions that you make in life and that includes what you get rid of and what you keep.
- Decide which area you are going to tackle first; the bathroom, the attic.
- Deal with things in small chunks. Categorize your items into small piles so you soon start to see a clarity shining through. Books, jewellery, clothes, DIY tools, accessories, antiques, furniture, upholstery, children's toys, educational matter.
- When you start to let go of those items that don't carry such a highly emotionally charge to them it becomes easy to let go.
- If you have things that are emotionally charged with feelings, memories, and parts of your life intertwined in them you have to let go – move them towards the entrance slowly but surely.

Gratitude is one way of overcoming some of these emotional obstacles. Be thankful for what you have and what you had. But realize it served its purpose and now it's time to create more space for new ideas and people.

If there are a lot of painful memories attached to an object, then the emotional energy attached to it is better out of the environment. Once you start to let go of these THINGS the power returns to YOU. You are no longer allowing these things stored to consume your space, time and energy. Being able to let go of it brings the POWER of choosing and deciding back to you. Many people are slaves of their matter allowing everything and anything into their domain. This is an ideal opportunity for you to become the king or queen of your own home.

- Be aware of how you feel as you bag up those old memories; the unnecessary items you have stored for yourself and others and let go of them. It is often accompanied with a mild loss but also a feeling of letting go and being light within you. It is not difficult to accrue clutter in this age of mass consumption and junk mail.

- The list below is what you can do with the different items you may need to let go of.

1. For all paper clutter shred it before disposing of it.

2. For clothes put in bags for charity shops,

3. If you have to let go of textiles, ceramics, beads you can present them to schools for art classes.

4. Items of value put to one side to be sold to Antique Dealers

5. Be aware of not holding onto items whilst waiting for them to be sold on the internet-you can offer them as free to be collected but you don't want the items staying any longer than required as this creates frustration and disheartenment.

6. Time frames; set forty-five minutes to focus totally and take fifteen minutes for a rest. Repeat

7. When you give things away you are creating more space within yourself, your life generally.

8. Deposit goods you are letting go of by your front door: this is a way of reminding yourself to let go. Every time you come home, you'll be reminded of what you need to remove from your home. Extraordinary change requires extraordinary action. Dependent on where you live you can take everything out of rooms and place it outside only allowing the must items back into the home.

STEP FOUR – TO FLOW OR TO FREEZE?

When moving house or clearing out the house people have a great idea; they put things they value into storage until they need them.

Having done this myself I spent £3000 in three years in storage fees and I don't know where any of the stuff is now.

7 Days To Transform Your Life

A client's mother died ten years ago. He put her furniture in storage and since then has spent £20.000 in fees. He's now homeless, sleeping in his taxicab. Let this be a cautionary tale that it is better to let go than to hold on to stuff that is going to physically, financially and emotionally weigh you down later on.

I pointed out that he needed to let go not only of the furniture but the sadness around the loss of his mother. I totally understand how difficult it is; I have been there and cleared out a house full of memories for a large family forty-four years living in one place.

This man had not moved on-he was going from pillar to post but would not surrender the storage even though the fees were crippling him. Now not everybody has this issue but often we have a small aspect of it. Some people don't want to let go of tangible items because somehow they have morphed into them, they are their memories, childhood, and identities-it is almost WHO THEY ARE!

Another guy had his garage jammed packed but some of the belongings were his ex-wife's – he wanted to meet someone new but he could not bear to clear out the garage and deal with the feelings associated with the content.

Remember Nikola Tesla said that everything is energy; all our acquisitions have an energy to them. However, when they start to gather dust, they also exude energy of brokenness and stagnancy.

Our items, physical acquisitions define who we think we are. How we perceive what is around us becomes our reality. Ensure you are the architect of your own S P A C E and that the meanings you perceive are the one's you want to pursue.

Ever been on a motorway and there is space in front of you, it does not remain empty for long. People want to fill up spaces all the time. The emptiness reflects back something deeper within us but that is where the difficulty is in letting go of the clutter. When you have space you have potential. Then you have to take responsibility.

Remember it's the space that defines Who You Are!

"The usefulness of the cup, is it's emptiness." – *Bruce Lee*

We all know what it is like as a child to go into a place or a space that is expansive. As children we have a softer and finer energy and pick up the essence of where we are and how it makes us feel.

So, this step is **NO MORE STORAGE**. It is like you are storing a part of yourself; and we crystallize if we psychologically know that a part of our identity (or what we deem to be us) is put away in a cold and darkened room. It's almost like being frozen for some time.

I had a client who reported how much she had cleared in her home including all the meat in the freezer that had been there for seven years! Is this what we are doing to ourselves? Storing away and freezing who we are- what we eat?

I would also like to remind you of how full our heads, and homes are of messages exuded by monitors, computers and smartphones. Our space is filled with invisible lines of communication and the impact on some people is that it fogs the mind causing confusion and conflict.

Our minds are full of information and decisions, and we become easily distracted by anything whether it is sounds, or words and forget what is most important; how we feel inside!! Peace cannot be bought, but we can create that within us.

Energetically we have become frozen in time. Our emotions and memories have resisted change. I know it is difficult to change for many but the only thing that is constant is change. You must go with the flow, but how can you do that when the flow is blocked by a lack of space?

Think of it like this: if you have a bad day or are not feeling well you would not want to be surrounded by clutter would you? Sometimes people feel safer in places where the web they have created for themselves no longer surrounds them.

That is why some people, from my experiences, feel safer in hospitals and do not want to return home to the turmoil in their own homes.

If you store stuff in the loft it represents the mind and the lack of clarity that exists. Stored in the cellar represents our deepest fears we choose not to address and tackle. Just clearing these out is like a rebirth.

Once you have cleared a space, sit back and congratulate yourself; after all you will have the space to see just how far you have come. Acknowledge how much of a difficult task it has been to do but you have made progress! You will also feel as light as a feather.

STEP FIVE– LETTING GO, LETTING FLOW, AND FINDING SPACE

The process of letting go is about being conscious of how it affects you. The nature of the mind is that it wants to fill the space with more things. This is about being awake and paying attention to how you are feeling, thinking and relaxing into the new space.

Where does all your "stuff" go? It can go to assist others it can go to the charity shops.

Letting go is yet again another habit that has to be created but have you noticed that once you have thrown one difficult thing out it becomes so much easier to keep throwing out and letting the things go go go. In fact, you start to throw everything out because having space makes you feel great and free!

If you live in a cluttered environment it tends to affect everything else you do. Letting go of one thing helps to let go of everything that needs to go.

Be mindful also that the mind creates distractions. The mind is fast like a knife and will do anything to sabotage the beauty of creating space on the inside and on the outside. So be more aware of how your thinking can self-defeat or self-sabotage.

You can say, "Thanks For Sharing But This Clearing Away Is Going To Happen Regardless."

Watch Out For Distractions Such As

- I Could Put Stuff On Ebay But Computer Is Broken So I Can't Do That

- I Am Waiting For Someone With A Car To Take It But They Are Never Available

- I Need Others To Make Decisions When In Reality They Won't Even Miss The Stuff

- I Am Tired, I Am Hungry, We All Find 1000 Excuses And More Not To Do The Unthinkable. Let Go.

- Beware of WEAPONS OF MASS DISTRACTION!

Undertaking this journey of letting go internally and externally you will more likely feel lighter, have greater clarity, more focus, greater creativity and more room to maneuver and space to invite greater vibes and feelings. Not to mention that you will actually have more Time to do the things you really want to do; you spend less time negotiating the clutter and being fogged by what surrounds you.

STEP 5 – NOW THAT WE FOUND SPACE-WHAT DO WE DO WITH IT?

It's one thing to create the space; it's another to maintain it.

Now that you have merged into an amazing space you have to continue to be mindful of what it is you are bringing in; how you change the habits and patterns of how you reside in your space. In this space comes a reflection of taking responsibility for your life; what you put into your space, how you use it and how you process it. It is the same for your mind-what do you feed your mind with; endless gossip, criticism, self-torture or beauty, kindness, and compassion?

The most important component in any change is creating a habit of self-discipline.

As Robert Kiyosaki says, **"Discipline delivers a higher quality of life."**

No matter what level of quality of life you prefer it is the same for all areas of your existence; self-discipline in what you choose to do, eat, absorb and create.

At this stage I would also like to err on the side of caution that whilst minimalism can be very alluring this whole subject of clutter is about maintaining balance within and without. So, to go to the total opposite is not balanced neither. Let me tell you why. I have also entered homes where I felt nobody lived there at all. There was no colour, no hint of life and yet individuals did live there but were devoid of an emotional balance.

STEP 6 – OTHER HIDDEN AREAS OF STAGNANCY

Besides the physical area we live in here are some other areas that subconsciously can affect our clarity of thinking and organization.

- PURSE OR WALLET - Somehow we become endowed with receipts, slips of paper, and articles. Suddenly it's bulging, but not with money. When you do a cleanse of all these items you feel lighter in yourself. You leave space symbolically for more cash/cards to enter.

- BAG – How many of us have carried our lives around us in one bag or two? If you go the gym, go running, have children with their needs considered you can often have the whole house in there. I have been committed to just emptying everything out in one space; then only that which is pertinent is allowed back inside.

- CAR – We don't realize how much we carry with us but operating out of a clear and undistracted car once again relaxes our muscles, mind and overall we feel we are not carrying the world on our shoulders.

- PHONE It's good to let go of the computer and the phones and be aware of how your responses and reactions change. You slowly let go of the instant reaction to look, hear and respond. Do we really need the ghosts of people's telephone numbers knowing that they are no longer in our life or are we pretending to think we will contact them

STEP 7 - YOUR LIFE DOES NOT IMPROVE BY CHANCE, BUT BY CHANGE, FENG SHUI CHANGE

When you have created space on the outside it has a direct correspondence with how you feel within. When there is space then there is less emotional, mental, and materialistic din influencing your decisions. You have clarity to see and feel exactly what you want and where you want to go or how you want to feel. Using your new-found space is like handing you a million dollars-why? Because everything around you from the invisible to the visible whether sounds, colours, orientation of space, pictures, aroma are obviously and subtly influencing how you feel about yourself; what you feel you are capable of; how you live your life, aspirations, possibilities and much more. Who is in your life is also part of that environment so be sure that you have chosen exactly who you want in that SPACE!

Once you have created your space by going through the process above and you have cleared the decks the next step is to clear the invisible patterns of feeling and thoughts when you go into any home or workplace. Through the Power of Space Cleansing you can prepare even more for the success, focus and delivery of your health, wealth and relationships. The techniques I discuss are an essential ingredient for anyone moving into a new property especially when they have just got married or living together; running a business from home, bringing up a family or having any health or healing issues.

Taking action (action points and exercises):

CLUTTER

Prepare for De-cluttering by Drawing a Plan

- ✧ So, get yourself some paper and pen;

- ✧ draw the area of your home or space

- ✧ prioritize which area is the most important and not forgetting that this is a process. You can colour code it by using red for the really urgent need to remove and blue and green for less urgent attention. See Clutter list in Index

- ✧ Identify what are the major items you want out of the home; could be furniture, mementoes,

2. Make A date as to when you are going to start and who will assist.

- ✧ Chunk your time. 45 minutes' work and 15 minutes to rest and take stock.

- ✧ The less emotional stuff can be castaway easily.

- ✧ For the more emotional stuff, be prepared to say to yourself that it was great whilst here but you cannot make any use of it now and to hang onto it clutters up valuable space

- ✧ See my tapping videos letting go of clutter at back index.

- ✧ Storage is frozen energy

- ✧ **Letting go; watch for distractions!**

✧ Beware of other people popping in and robbing your time whilst doing very important shifting work

✧ Beware of others in the house who want you to keep everything because within themselves they cannot make the space to let go

✧ Do not put the T.V. on or pick up phones to have conversations and then you are half way through your process then it is never completed

✧ Make the time special by turning off all devices and focus on this task

✧ Go to my YouTube channel Cathi Hargaden for a series of videos about changing the energy through de-cluttering

✧ Manage the space you have created; Do not be tempted to fill it up!

✧ Once you have cleared out a room, area, garage, or cupboards be aware of your mind telling you that you need to refill it with more stuff

✧ Enjoy the space and feel how it changes your thinking and feelings

7. Move to celebrate the accomplishment with gratitude and your own power within.

✧ Now you have space to dance, sing, exercise in that place that feels more expansive

---

✧ Having a house warming party to celebrate the new space as that always injects a new energy into the home.

✧ For those who would still like to have assistance in this matter you can contact me for Skype calls or consultations: www.wealthyspaces.com

---

DAY 2 – SPACE CLEANSING

1. What is Space Cleansing?

Have you ever found yourself in a place which just did not feel quite right? What about a house you have thought of buying or renting but it did not feel at ease? Or those other places where the smell, emptiness, or atmosphere stopped you from going any further. Then there are other dwellings which made you feel abundant, elevated as soon as you walk in the door – enough to make you want to move in right there and then. You are using all your senses and intuition to pick up on how something may feel to you even though it cannot be tangibly felt or seen.

Energy patterns are created all the time by the way we think, what actions we do, and how we consciously and unconsciously design to plan our own lives. In doing this we create patterns in the way we think, feel and do. Some of these can be very positive or negative; yin and yang; patterns are inevitably left by all of us.

It is almost like spinning our own web and especially in places where we live do patterns begin to manifest. That is why when you go into a house someone has lived for any length of time you will sense or feel a certain kind of atmosphere; the thoughts and feelings we have become absorbed into the atoms around us; be it brick, furniture, or curtains. If there has been a lot of animosity, fear, abuse, or torture it is often picked up and interpreted as a repellant to wanting to be there. Everyone leaves behind energy because we are all operating from various frequencies and resonances from what we say, do, feel and exude. These patterns are not just the domain of peoples' personal residences but also refer to work places, areas where people have been tortured or imprisoned. There is a resistance for people to be around spaces that do not feel great for example hospitals, prisons and places of misfortune. There are ways of dissipating those patterns and this is what I mean by cleansing a space. It can be something as simple as using the elements of nature; Earth or fire to shake up these patterns eventually allowing them to be consumed and/or dissipated.

Space cleansing is integral to people protecting themselves from other peoples' negativity. In the beginning cultures and communities used the idea of protecting themselves and safety has been the most important component of survival. Whether it be physical protection or psychic protection, mankind has always sought a way and means of guarding itself by building castles, fences and brick walls to keep people out as well as to keep people confined.

Besides the obvious reasons being safe and survival, the other aspect of protection has been for psychic defense. Personally it took me a long time to realize that this kind of attack actually exists. If we go on the premise that thoughts have power, then a lot of the time peoples' thoughts are projected outwards towards others. That is quite normal, of course, but when those thoughts become destructive, a certain force, a weapon against the mental and emotional cloud of other peoples' existence, it can manifest harm in many forms.

It was not until I had been on quite a few journeys across the world that I started asking questions about some of the most grotesque architecture that was positively unfriendly and unsavory to the eye.

With a reverence for other cultural histories, I accepted what was in front of me as integral to the culture I was visiting until I started to see a pattern occurring right across the world.

What was the pattern? Here are just some of the features I noticed;

✧ in India in the temples certain symbols like salt hanging from the beams

✧ outside on the front paths geometric designs

✧ some of the native American Indian structures like totem poles had significant animals on them designed to protect

✧ the gothic features in Europe are all warding off something that is often invisible to the eye.-those nasty looking creatures projecting from buildings

Whilst some cultures are far more aware of the unwanted feelings and thoughts directed at them and consult a witch doctor, priest, rabbi or imam, in society generally people experience conflicts or what is perceived as bad luck and never wonder about the power behind it.

Space cleansing therefore, is a recognition that webs and patterns of energy exist which give us feelings that can be uncomfortable or threatening. For whatever reason these patterns can exude heaviness, sadness, tragedy or loss. It is not to say that there are not places with great happiness. Even so it is still good to cleanse all spaces making way for your own great patterns of energy. To space cleanse a property is to acknowledge the existence of patterns creating a feeling which you want to dissolve. Below is a process on how to do this yourself.

2. PROTECTION

Space-cleansing has not always been a sacred gesture done as part of a ritual, but rather as an extension of domestic cleansing.

Not that long ago in the UK in street after street of terraced homes it was a very common sight to see the women cleaning the front steps and pavement that led to their homes. It was a form of cleansing and preventing what was coming in from the outside and bringing the bad feeling on to the inside.

In other cultures, notably with an Islamic background it is fundamental to take off one's shoes before entering the main atrium of the home; the soles of the shoes have the dirt of the world and as a home is like a temple one would not want to bring that inside.

Much of the Arabic architecture when you look through the front door it is impossible to see right through as there is a wall that impedes the vision of what is inside – designed to keep the evil eye away from the residents, particularly the women inside.

So here we have architecture and daily ritual as part of suspending any unwanted focus from outsiders onto the energy of the inner atrium of people's welfare and wellbeing.

The entrances to most buildings are where protectors are placed from unwanted chi – unwanted thoughts, emotions and intentioned bad will.

Throughout India, Bali and many other nations the symbolism at the front entrances was stridently similar; frightening-looking creatures on the outsides of the temples were all a reminder of creating fear of any ill will or attack.

One of the resources for protection has been the use of rice to be laid out in front of the building; rice was always a symbol of wealth in China but in India it was used as a means of absorbing malcontent energy. If there is a new home or a new business, a bowl of rice is put outside to harness any negative chi and allow the good energies to enter the building. The photograph below was found outside a hotel recently but the same idea is also used in ceremonies to protect when opening a new business or home.

These rituals may appear superstitious but some have well-grounded practicality to them. In any room or space, aromas and moisture hang in the air. The moisture or water holds a memory, of what has happened in that space. The energy of thought according to and illustrated by Dr Emoto is captured in water molecules. Imagine when you walk into a room you cannot see water but you can feel an energy. It can be any thought pattern but if it has not been cleansed it can be negative over time and is suspended in the atmosphere. Nobody ever knows what has gone on behind closed doors regardless of wealth, culture, or location. Epsom salts scattered around the corners and skirting boards of rooms act as an absorber of unwanted chi. Rice is another absorber of moisture placed in bowls around the home this can be thrown away after a few days. If not rice, use sea salt and leave for a couple of weeks in bowls in each room. This process is good to do especially moving into a new home, business or if there has been strife within your own life.

We have all entered places and spaces where it visually looked right but the feeling was not good at all. What is hanging in the air to create this feeling? Most people don't care to find out or they allow their visual sense of apparent cleanliness and bright colours to distract them from their sixth sense of feeling; if we sharpened up that feeling we would be able to detect that despite the apparent allure of a nice place the feeling is not congruent.

Another aspect of protecting a space is some of the figures integral to buildings and statues. These statues were designed deliberately to ward off unwanted attention. They are to be found pulling out their tongues and disfiguring their faces and bodies to scare off any strangers or unwanted attention.

65

Some of the statues/postures are profoundly non-inviting – quite scary and horrific – the rationale behind it is don't bring your bad luck or unwanted negative chi in here.

When I lived in Greece I could not comprehend this idea of the evil eye, and worn by everyone in the village in Crete. The evil eye symbol was found everywhere in the homes and shops I entered.

It wasn't until much later in my life that I realized the power and the thinking behind it was to ward off bad luck and unwanted thoughts and feelings of strangers and friends alike.

The evil eye is found throughout Greece, Cyprus and Turkey, but other countries have their own versions of it.

Throughout my travels I identified other places where they hailed designs outside the front door as in Kerala, India. The house I was living in was just built and they hung a large salt pod, aloe vera and a Kerala symbol of protection outside the home.

Other cultures hang dried rosemary and other herbs—a common phenomenon used throughout France in previous centuries. Rosemary was believed to have an aroma that warded off people and undesirable "spirits". Rosemary and tea tree were used in hospitals up until 1920s, as it was believed to absorb the energies within the ward of sadness and loss but at the time primarily used to stop infection during those periods.

During the great plague, doctors and lawyers would wear large beaked bird masks stuffed with herbs to protect them from infections but also unwanted and negative chi.

So we can see from this that mankind has always wanted to protect itself from invisible forces that could potentially manifest bad circumstances.

Whether this is all hocus pocus to you, the reality is that energy and vibrations create patterns of thinking and feeling. If untoward thoughts and feelings come your way, isn't it better to protect yourself than leave yourself exposed?

The opposite set of thoughts and feelings is to be found in William Wattles' book in The Science of Getting Rich where he deems the thoughts, feelings and mindset and visualization of what you create or want must precede manifestation. See Day 5 where we put this into action!

This was recently found outside the entrance to many a house and it was explained to me that it was a pentacle to ward off unwanted and malevolent thoughts.

Feng Shui has its own form of protection through the use of the bagua mirror. These mirrors have the symbols of ancient energy patterns and depending upon whether you are repelling or attracting something to you will determine which mirror you use.

The bagua mirror can have a concave shape which allures only the best energies into that front door. Others have a convex shape repelling unwanted chi into that household. Others are flat mirrors basically ascribing the principle of the divine energy to protect the house from tragedy whether it be health, finance or anything else.

3. DIFFERENT PROCEDURES

Here are just some of the practices that are available to you for cleansing a space you intend to live or work in.

That space can be anywhere-I mean people say to me oh it's all nonsense, it's rubbish, but they are the very people that seek out great locations, nice places to live and would prefer to live in environments that exude the best vibrations.

If you have been in and out of properties like I have done for housing associations, government houses, private houses, hospitals and luxury houses then you know what it's like when a place makes you feel a certain way. It doesn't have to be in a not-so-good area; any space is subject to bad things happening that create patterns over a period of time and know that when you walk in, it does not feel right. It's all down to how you are made to feel.

Even people living in beautiful houses with beautiful locations can be affected by the energy that is negative within their own four walls. Because patterns have not been cleared, conflict, negativity build up and this becomes the feeling or atmosphere of the room regardless of how wealthy the location or house is. Whole streets or areas have patterns of repeating the same problems over and over again from ill fated health to divorce and tragedy.

These procedures are for everyone! They would benefit countless landlords who fail to get that people leave behind a trail of energetic debris and then they wonder why the same bad tenants continue to be attracted to the same property. Or issues arise suddenly and they think it has nothing to do with the space in which they live. If those who rent out properties carried out this approach they would be most likely to have a different energetic tenant entering the property.

No matter whether you are renting, purchasing or sharing your living space from time-to-time you need to cleanse it enough to clear the air. If you have had conflict in the home, bad news, or losses then it is best to cleanse the space so psychologically you feel you are starting afresh and are going to feel different.

Protect yourself at your front entrance but don't go making a fort to imprison yourself. Have a welcoming entrance but just protect yourself; basically get a balance, which is what Feng Shui is all about. The business of balancing your life through your environment is a serious one.

Before trying out some of the procedures below, I suggest you sit where you are and close your eyes and breathe steadily. Be as still as possible and feel what it is you feel in this space now. After you have taken action on some of the ideas below, sit down again and see what feels differently for you.

4. SPACE CLEANSING PROCEDURES

For those who understand this concept, there are certain steps you can actively take to physically and psychologically cleanse a space. The following are just some of the ways you can get started and the photos illustrate some of the tools you can access right away.

Basic tool can be smoke and fire. Fire is the element used traditionally to cleanse a space and break down any patterns in the atmosphere. An incense stick would be a good place to start wafting behind doors, into corners and space that feels stagnant or dead.

- Use a ceramic burner with a blend of oils that pervade the atmosphere, which not only offers an aroma but also sustains and changes the atmosphere.

- Rosemary and juniper with lemon essential oils are excellent air cleansers to be used first thing in the morning only. The reason for this is because these oils are stimulants so you do not want to use them in the evening as they will keep you awake.

- Participating in these procedures is best done before 2 p.m.-preferably in morning as the energy changes with the direction of the light and intensity of the sun throughout the day. It also leaves time to dispose of the dissipated smoke and chi from the windows of that room.

- Use a sage stick or smudging stick in and around the home and especially in areas where there is stagnancy. This is called smudging, an ancient tradition used to cleanse old-set patterned energies. Use of charcoal burners with resins such as benzoin, myrrh and frankincense placed on the burning coal have a lasting sweeping effect through the atmosphere-it leaves behind a favourable resin aroma. The precautions and how to do this method of cleansing is discussed here on my YouTube channel: Cathi Hargaden. In Dubai they sell wood chips that have been absorbed with aromas like oud used for centuries to clear out old wounds and spaces where people have resided.

✧ Sound waves have always been used as a means of cleansing spaces. In ancient times the town crier used sound to bring news. Church bells are used to bring people to church. Tibetan bells and singing bowls are used for hypnosis, focus and to cleanse the surrounding environment. That is why music is hypnotic and magnetic because the geometry of the beat meets a pattern and frequency within a space and changes the atmosphere. Some of the traditional modes of sound have been pure—just clapping of hands in corners and waking up the stagnancy of rooms, corners and areas of the house never visited.

✧ Go to my YouTube Channel for my videos where I talk to Angar who teaches how to use the Tibetan singing bowls. The sound waves from the various size, make and design of the bowls determines the sound that affects the vibrations and frequencies of the space.

✧ Putting on the best vibrant classical music to shift the low-base energy left behind by negative partners, visitors, guests or even yourself. Because of the frequency of certain music it takes away base-low level frequencies.

5. SIMPLER METHODS

For those not wanting to demonstrate the above methods the more subtle means of cleansing a space can be many and below are just a few suggestions:

- Place bowls of vinegar and lemon in and around the rooms which can help act as an astringent on the atmosphere

- Bowls of rock salt left for a few weeks will absorb water from the atmosphere-after three weeks throw away the salt as it will have absorbed the patterns of moisture

- Orange and lemon peel in hot water in a bowl to absorb the dryness in the atmosphere dispelling old and established patterns.

- Oils of juniper, sage, frankincense and bergamot to burn in each of the rooms to take away and dissipate those patterns.

- Buy a bag of rice and go along all your skirting boards and corners and let the rice flow from the bag as though sand and leave behind a trail of rice – leave it for a few days. What it is doing is absorbing low and slow energetic debris the kind of vibrations hoovers/vacuums cannot move. I was commissioned by a medical doctor to do this for her new house because she knew this ancient practice had a cleansing meaning behind it.

Finally, when you have gone through these processes:

1. Whether you are using smudging, incense, carbon with resin or wood chips move around the room going into corners, top shelves and areas that have been dormant wafting the incense. Whilst doing this engage your thoughts with the intention that you are willing to let go or that you are thanking the space for what it has provided up to now and you're creating more space for greater abundance to enter the space.

2. When leaving the premises, windows should still be closed.

3. After two to three hours return to the space and open all the windows ensuring all smoke has left the premises. Usually most smoke alarms do not go off. Please ensure they work before and after procedures, as this is essential for your own safety.

4. Also, all carbon resins, incense sticks, and candles must be put out before leaving the premises-don't leave them smouldering. I have made mistakes-learn from them.

5. Incense can continue to be used, as can aromatic oils. You can use the essential oils to create a mood for relaxation or a feeling of a new vibration in that space with essential oils such as frankincense, geranium, lime, and benzoin.

6. A more passive way of generating great energy is to have a crystal hanging in or near a window where light shines through into your home. Even whilst you are out it is a great pleasure to return to the home with the rainbows all around the walls of your room – this uplifts and generates a great mood after a long day at work.

Be aware of how clearing the air makes you feel; be vigilant about what it is you notice and how that impacts upon your life. If anything, you often feel cleared from within just purely by doing the cleansing and sweeping away what you have to let go of.

6. CELEBRATION

Realise that taking the time out to actually do this ritual is in itself a blessing to the space. Now it's time to celebrate the letting go of the old and inviting the new vibe you want into your life. You can say goodbye to the old stuff and awaken the new within.

7. OUTCOMES AND BENEFITS

There are many outcomes when finalizing this procedure dependent on what you started with. I know that having been in over 2000 homes the low ebb energy, stagnancy, blockage and misery experienced can be dispersed if people were awakened to the fact that something needs to change.

7 Days To Transform Your Life

Often we know deep within us we need to change something in our lives but we don't know what or we don't know how. That alone can be such a frustrating experience. But rather than tackle something you are not quite sure about, changing the next best thing is what I have suggested on Day 2.

This procedure is often one way to symbolically and functionally start to make changes by sweeping away the old patterns and starting afresh. It allows us to:

- Remove the blocks and lack of flow within the environment

- Generate a different energy

- Attract a different vibration

- Shift our own vibrational aura and then focus on what we want to attract ourselves.

- Shift our own self-sabotaging patterns to create new and positive patterns in and around us.

- It is essential to start with the right mood and feeling beforehand.

Please note that there is no point at all in undertaking the above direction if you have not cleared the clutter in your space. To assist you with the space clearing procedure contact Cathi on http://www.wealthyspaces.com for consultation, your own space-clearing box, tools to get started, assistance or Skype discussion.

Taking action (action points and exercises):

1. **PREPARATION** – Get a feeling of what you are picking up in and around your space.

2. **DO** – Purchase incense stick, packet of rice, Epsom salts, smudge stick, vinegar and lemon, or essential oils of rosemary and juniper.

3. Place vinegar and lemon juice into bowls in each room.

4. Sprinkle rice or Epsom salts around the skirting boards and corners to be cleaned up after 24 hours.

5. Burn the essential oils in a burner but only in the morning.

6. Burn the incense sticks walking around the rooms in and out of corners and behind doors only in the morning.

7. Place bowls of salt in each room is an alternative to the bowls of vinegar.

Get yourself a singing bowl and move around the house as shown in the videos on my YouTube channel –Cathi Hargaden.

You can get your Magic Space Clearing Box Available on www.wealthyspaces.com

8. Play some great music to wake up the energy of the space.

9. Sit back down, close your eyes and notice what a difference that has all made to how you feel – do this 24 hours after finished.

DAY 3 – INNER FENG SHUI

Inside Out Feng Shui is about going within ourselves to shift the perceptions of our reality on the outside. Wherever thought goes energy flows so what is coming from us we have to make sure we design and sculpt the best vision for ourselves. We cannot just focus on the change on the outside and that is why this day is going to be the bridge between letting go of the energetic debris we cleared the first two days, to sitting on Day 3 to do some inner cleansing and shifting so you are ready for the changes you want to manifest in your environment and your life.

Through the power of meditation and relaxation it's possible to discover what we truly want for ourselves, what is important and what we would like to change. An understanding of the five elements/energies that exist within us, are pivotal to the concepts of change, balance and vibrational energies that we exude as individuals. This in turn then affects our environments and interactions with others.

To understand what I am about to write you have to look at your life in terms of metaphor and symbol, archetype and mythology - because often this is the only way we can not only get to understand our worlds but also use what lies within us. Some of our thoughts and feelings are so deep, contorted, a mixture of where we have come from, the environments we live in and the people that we have surrounding us, as well our nutrition, that to express them in a limited amount of words would be impossible. This is why there are so many mythical great stories, symbolic journeys from Alice in Wonderland, King Minos and The Minotaur of Crete, they are all about returning back to the centre – that is our true home. The Wizard of Oz, Jason and the Argonauts, Pans Labyrinth, and Gulliver's Travels are all telling a story about the rich textures of our inner life. It is a way of navigating a story that has meaning to our own journeys internally but ultimately all these stories talk about returning home – and that home is ultimately within YOU. As children are growing up, they have an internal world of their own. It is a hidden cavern of insights, tales and rich visions and curiosities that stay within. That is why we have mythologies, fantasy worlds to symbolize a journey we travel internally and how we survive the inner conflicts and the highs and lows of our lives. Today offers an opportunity to explore the inner architecture in a curious manner; clearing out old stuff and making space internally for new concepts, perceptions and visions for the reality you would prefer to attract in your life.

Day 3 is about change and alchemy on the inside. We are going to use techniques that will help us get clearer on a vision internally, relax into acceptance, open the windows and doors within us and breathe in a more vibrant energy. Each step will allow more insight into helping you make changes for yourself. Let's get started.

1. TECHNIQUES TO STILL YOU

All health comes from the quality of your breathing. Not just for the physical health but for clarity of thinking, outlook and seeing life through a different pair of glasses.

To look at the internal flow of chi is to look at the essence of why you are alive. No breath, no life! Yet we pay so little attention to this daily act. Breathe measures your levels of anxiety, stress, and relaxation, and the more you take time out to breathe deeply, the more your quality of life is positively affected. As an Occupational Therapist I see many limbs amputated because the smaller arteries and capillaries in the extremities have no oxygen. Once again the concept of flow is blocked from within.

What stops us from breathing in a way that affects our lives for the better? Pure habit in the way we sit, our posture, laziness – and lack of awareness. Most people are driving but there is no driver in the car. Ever gone to work in the morning in the car and arrived and wondered how you got there?

So over a lifetime we build up rhythms, habits and patterns that are never questioned and we call this OUR IDENTITY- this is who we think we are. However, this doesn't mean that once the patterns have been established over a lifetime you cannot change them. The difference is you have to want to change them. Some people make a conscious effort to change their habits and lifestyles. For others at times the pain has gotten to be too much, the crushing defeat turns to surrender, the realization that there is nowhere else to go and you have to change your perception of your reality. if you go to My YouTube channel; Cathi Hargaden, meditations, visualizations you can start to use them.

So how do we get started?

First of all, find yourself a quiet space to sit in your clutter-free area cleared home or office. Ensure it doesn't have any distractions around and it's comfortable. Once seated be still.

These breathing meditations create a space for you internally. They clear the cobwebs, let go of the dross, and make a space for new experiences to come into your life. Letting go of the clutter inside is a must. Your House is you and your inner architecture. Try the following:

- Breathe in for the count of four; hold for count of four and slowly breathe out for eight. As you push the breath out through your nose let all the clutter come out with it.

- Breathe in through one nostril whilst with ring finger and thumb closing the other nostril. Then close both nostrils and take your finger and thumb away and breathe out through the other nostril. Then repeat five to ten times. This is tantamount to cleansing yourself daily from within. When breathing is deliberate it creates more oxygen to the brain and thereby elevates you, naturally allowing all poisonous and useless thought patterns to breakdown; hence a breathing session a day keeps the psychiatrist and the anti-depressants away!!

Breathing is the essence of your life so if you are breathing in fumes from a poor environment this affects not only your lungs but also your capacity to function intellectually & emotionally. Besides the physical advantages the psychological benefits are that when space is given to you it creates a distance and a different perspective. It is because there is no space in peoples' lives that they react the way they do. Not just physical space but the psychological space within. Breathing deeply is a form of space clearing. We let go of the cobwebs and the strains and stresses within. Space clearing is essential for creating fresh space within us so we can receive more positive patterns that support us in our daily lives.

The breathing technique can develop into a meditation practice by just being still and relaxing. You have created space within yourself sufficiently to Let Go! I have to tell you from my experience that each time you do this it is different; it becomes a form of space cleansing from within. It's like cleaning your internal windows when you breathe, focus and stay still and let go. Each time you do this, you can see out of clearer windows in which you view the world; your perceptions, clarity, focus and creativity become sharper allowing you to live a more fulfilled life – day by day.

I am not going to pretend that your thoughts do not come rushing into that space initially as though you are the last bus out of the city and they have to get on board! The mind counts on you giving up. That's right. Who would sit with all those thoughts and emotions, best tuck them under the bed and in the loft – keep them at bay. It is not about resolving the thoughts but more allowing them to come and pass so you are sufficiently distant, sitting in a space just allowing them to pass by.

SEE ACTIONS AT END OF CHAPTER WHAT CAN YOU DO?

2. VISUALISATION OF LETTING GO INSIDE.

The power of using your mind's eye is to go inside and create a feeling and a perception that allows all the dross of life to be filtered out.

Visualize a garden, for example. It involves colour, aroma and texture. We seldom use our imaginations to create pictures we want to experience as increasingly entertainment is created for us by other peoples' perceptions.

Within the corridors of our own minds there are rooms that have never been entered; the kind of rooms that can offer you good health, peace and harmony. The windows are dirty and there is grunge from the past. The corners are full of cobwebs and the doors are creaking with the lack of attention. The pipes are noisy as the flow sputters and coughs whilst somewhere deep within lies a space where there are no noises, movement or conflict and this is the space we will create within by the end of the book.

In the visualization you can focus on your forehead between both eyes and create a space there; then practice letting go of situations,

Take the road to **Letting Go** because if you don't you get pile up inside!!

What Can You Do?

If you go to my YouTube channel there are meditations there for visualizing with colour, homes, and gardens, relating to our organs which relate to the five symbolic elements of our existence.

Creating a healing space within your home just for YOU allows the doorway into your internal world to be given some light. I have a webinar "**7 Feng Shui Steps to a Healthier Life**" which can help you create a self-healing space on my website: www.wealthyspaces.com

Here are the Seven Top Tips for Creating your Sacred Silent Space

1. Find a place where you can sit comfortably and undisturbed. Bring in a textured blanket or cover and choose a colour that is not busy but is calming.

2. Make sure there are no distractions around you – take away laptops – leave the phone in the other room on airplane mode. Your peace of mind is more important than any casual calls.

3. If you are okay with aromas you can create a calming aroma of frankincense, benzoin and bergamot.

4. If this is a space you wish to return to again you could place a picture that is calming to the eye so when you gaze at it you associate it with a good feeling for you.

5. Ensure there is air circulating sufficiently so you do not veer towards nodding off.

6. One or two pink rose quartz crystals has a calming effect associated with the emotions. Place one in each hand.

7. Discipline yourself so that each day you can afford at least ten minutes of putting your own needs first.

3. CLEANSING SOUNDS

Some rooms within us have never heard any sounds. Often our voices are not heard after we leave school. How many continue to sing, debate, express ourselves through the power of voice! Our vibrations of what is inside of us are illustrated in the sounds, tones of our words, thinking and voices. Whatever the vibrations of what we are thinking, saying to ourselves inside has a vibrational effect on the outside. The different vowel sounds resonate and make their own sound in each part of the body. Try expressing the sounds of the vowels on the diagram below.

It's the reason why people love music. It resonates in different parts of the body having a relaxing –stimulating effect upon the cells-nerve cells.

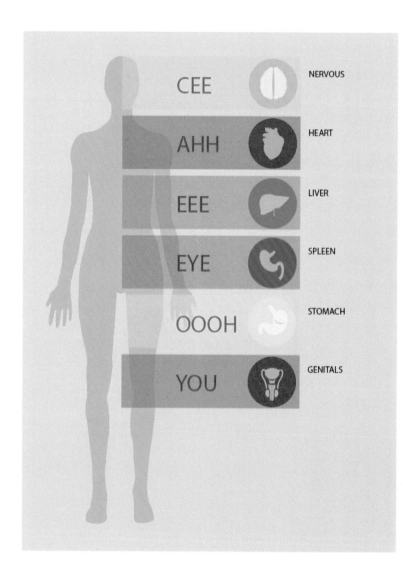

In the diagram have a go at saying the different sounds as they are written phonetically – one of the obvious sounds is the heart sound of AHH. We often use this sound for empathizing and agreement with our sentiments from the Heart Chakra. I heard this many times in the health environments. When you are saying this sound out loud you are resonating with the emotions of the heart.

If you practice saying CEE out loud – where are you picking up that sound within? You will find that it resonates above the neck area in the brain area. You are viewing the world from the brain area with two eyes and the third eye between the eyebrows.

The sound of EEE resonates and affects the liver. Say it and feel it in that area of your body. Often the sound we make when we are displeased and in disagreement, and this is what the liver does. It filters out what the body no longer needs or is in disagreement with.

The EYE sound is for the spleen. The spleen is important in the creation of the white blood cells and immunizing our bodies from harm. Our very immune system protects our existence. To express eye –I is emphasizing your very presence in the world.

When you say OOOH notice your stomach and intestines need to move and expand. Remember the intestines are said to be our second brain and where we feel our gut reacts to situations we experience in life. OOOH is a sound that beats all the way to the intestines and is an expression of a feeling in response to an environment outside of you.

The sound of saying YOU vibrates to the lower genital regions. Say a few times out loud. It is a sound that resonates all the way to the base chakra and reverberates to the genital area from which all life begins.

Imagine the sounds affecting us all the time on monitors, TVs and the radio. They are all insidiously influencing our inner peace and calm. Certain music has been known to hypnotize people into a certain state of being; it can be used as a form of social control as well as a manipulation of emotions and higher mental activity.

The sounds of dolphins are tracked by the sonar waves of sound in the water. Recently eighty large whales lost their direction and washed up dead on the beaches of Scotland. Experts speculated that sonar interference resulted in the whales losing their way. Sounds and messages on the outside can interfere with our own inner truths allowing the noise to drown out our own needs, our own inner voices.

Being exposed to certain musical sounds gives an edge to a child's development; it exposes him/her to vibrations and a resonance that can change the frequency within their own bodies. Listening to harp music or classical music will have a different resonance to that of rock music.

The power of sound has influenced how the architecture of buildings radiate a vibrancy and responds to the use of instruments and the human voice. Cathedral ceilings affects the resonance and vibration of that building. The acoustics then affects our own internal being so there is a feeling of becoming elevated with the sounds.

Likewise, within us, we too resonate and vibrate based on the timbre of our voice and expression of sounds. We have the opportunity to express the sounds too through music, acting, and conversations. Mantras are a group of sounds that creates differing effects upon our body; some affect us mentally, emotionally and assist with a different focus altogether.

There are powerful resonances of Tibetan singing bowls used for centuries to create and align frequencies within us and outside of us. One of the traditions used is to change the energy of water through the sounds made within singing bowls as a health nutrient. That means drinking the water in the bowl that has resonated from the sounds of the vibrational bowls.

All sounds grow into words; words are used to hypnotize our minds to generate a feeling or create an action. Therefore the words you choose to listen to and how you hear them, i.e. repeated words and what words you are saying to yourself, constitute a self-speak which also creates an energy about yourself. Therefore choosing affirmations that support you in your life are very powerful. The natural flow within, where we listen to our own inner truths are disrupted by the noise on the outside, we become confused. We have subliminal messages more often or not used for hypnotizing or manipulating masses of people.

We were children at one time where we were taught to repeat over and over words that did not make any sense to us but we did as we were told. You may want to consider phrases, words and passages you learned to quote as a young child and, whilst they may not have made much sense to you at the time they nevertheless had their own resonance and vibration which in turn would be effecting us as young children. This would be one way of influencing our belief systems, our identities as well as our limitations. Therefore, what is around us, what have we been saying to ourselves repeatedly affects our internal mindset especially in a negative manner. Therefore, this can be considered clutter of the mind that we have hung onto over the years. Does this stuff need clearing out from within?

What can you do?

I have used mantras with many students and the results have been amazing; mantras are not just any old letters thrown together they usually have been crafted together to create a sound internally and thereby affecting the overall resonance and vibration of yourself.

You can try out some of these sounds for yourself to see how it impacts upon your inner self; LOM CEE is one mantra; it's very simple; you repeat this sound over and over in your own mind, pronouncing it clearly. It is designed to create an emotional balance from within.

What is the best affirmation for you? Design affirmations shaping your positive thoughts– record them on your phone and repeat them daily. A program of generating good feelings for you will counter all the destructive messages being heard on the outside. Example: I am open to all the best business opportunities to me in my daily activities.

✧ Thank you for the amazing recovery of my health and my wealth.

✧ Thank you for the most amazing opportunities provided to me daily.

✧ Another way of affirming an idea of yourself is to write it down and put it up where you spend the most time – providing that it is safe to do so the message is reflected back to you at all times. (See DAY 5)

FOUR. Healing from within: Cells, Organs, and Vibrations

If you want to understand the power of Feng Shui internally then remember what Tesla said about energy, vibration and frequency. This is also true of what is exuding from every cell within us. What relationship do we have with any aspects of our internal workings, really? Our bodies are an amazing neurological piece of wiring and chemically designed to help us have hundreds of automatic activities going on simultaneously.

How do we perceive the organs, the cells that makeup those organs, the circulation of our fluids both red and white? How do we relate to ourselves on not only the physical and visual level but on emotional levels?

Our internal worlds are really the true undiscovered galaxies whether it is physiologically or spiritually. Would it really be so crazy to talk to these cells and organs and offer a gratitude that their finest of chemistries, tenacity to be like clockwork twenty-four hours daily continue to provide a service, an environment to yourself that honours your own greater being?

Let's say thanks to each major organ and create a driveway from the conscious mind into the depths of our working body. Would there possibly be an effect to our wellbeing? Why don't you try it and see?

Using some of these exercises the feedback from people who said yes to the above was one of huge shifts internally taking them to a different emotional or mental and physical disposition. The amazing power of the mind to heal and combat stress from within is well known

In order to heal from broken doors and smashed windows within ourselves there is often a solution. Does the solution lie in the synthetic and sophisticated retuning of chemicals that can change the experience of the mind of that person? These chemicals offer a solution for some but for many they begin to create secondary and tertiary symptoms, which often feel worse than the original symptom. For example, the huge amount of people who have been given pain killers or high blood pressure medication only for that very medication to turn into other problems like addiction to pain killers or affecting the organs.

An example would be one client taking medicine for epilepsy and instead of reducing the amount of fits his body became an internal firebomb burning his skin from the inside out!

So, what is it we can do to help and heal ourselves before inviting the onslaught of toxic chemical cocktails into our systems?

As mentioned previously about water-holding memory is it possible that our thought and emotional patterns can be held in suspension within the water content of our bodies? Muscles also hold memory, for every emotion it becomes a recording where our physical pain has an emotional precursor to it. Do our thoughts and feelings influence the physical? We have billions of cells that make up our bodies from skin to the major organs and it's not until something gives way, breaks down on the highway of our inner selves do we realize we have no connection or relationship with our inner environments.

Everything is focused on the outside – the entertainment of the world is all pulling us away from the most magical beauty of all; our internal selves both physically like a Swiss watch and spiritually like a galaxy beyond all stars.

To harness the power of within we have to connect with the cells that make up all the major organs of the body. For healing purposes below is a visualization you can use to connect on a cellular level using the power of healing colour and visualization.

People can visualise whatever colours are helpful for them to calm down and heal. I often use green or lime for the liver, blue for the kidneys, turquoise for the throat, white iridescent mother of pearl colour for the lungs, pink for the heart, yellow for the intestines and orange for the stomach. Purple for higher brow, gold for the feet. These colours can all be converted into pastel shades and all designed to calm and create a peaceful environment within.

VISUALISATION EXERCISE

You can also go to Cathi Hargaden YouTube Channel to listen to this visualization.

VISUALISATION FOR ORGANS

Become comfortable where you are sitting. Relax and let go of the whole of the body as though surrendering your physical body to the chair. Mentally and emotionally allow yourself to float those thoughts and feelings out of your attention to enable you to feel much lighter from within.

Now I'd like you to look deep inside of yourself and take your attention to the kidneys area of your body. As you look closer, you see the millions of cells that make up these organs. As you take a closer look you see that each cell has a face that looks sufficiently relaxed. Each of these thousands of cells are floating on water, the happier they are the more they chill out. The cells are floating in the most beautiful blue crystal waters the kind you get in a fresh spring or a deep blue sea. The kidney area deals with our innate fears and insecurities but because you are bathed in the blue crystal colour the fear is washed away. This allows your body to relax and let go of any residual fear you are holding onto. Be aware of allowing this part of your body letting go as though there is a floating experience within.

Next bring your attention to your liver, which lies underneath the right rib cage. As you become closer to this organ once again there are thousands of cells to protect you from poisonous substances and they filter out waste. As you see these cells you notice they have a tiny face on each cell; their faces smiling. The cells are bathing in the most amazing emerald green like the fields outside; they are vast, fresh and awe-inspiring. This organ, with all of its cells, tries to process emotions such as anger and bitterness. Go inside and observe the cells of this organ letting go of all tensions, tightness, and contradictions within.

Go to the lungs and observe the thousands of cells that make up this organ, which keeps your body filled with sufficient oxygen to keep all the functions going. As you zoom in to these lungs or lung, and, observe as you become closer to all the tiny cells that make up the lungs each has a face with a relaxed state; you see each cell is deeply breathing in and holding and gently and steadily letting go. The white iridescent pearled colour is shimmering within as you take deep breaths the shimmers become even greater. As you see each of these cells taking in deep breaths you feel your whole body taking in deep breaths, holding and gently letting go.

The organ of the heart and the blood that surrounds it carries millions of red vibrant cells. Focus on the heart area, as you become closer you see each cell has a face with great vitality, dynamism and power. These cells are all on top form, working well together, following the flow around the body and flow smoothly around bends and down tubes. Each of these cells all have a bright smile on their faces, happily laughing and enjoying life. They are pink, calming and exude a softness that mellows your feelings with an acceptance.

And finally, focus on the area of the stomach. Here once again there are millions of cells and as you see them closer and closer they have a yellow aura around them. Each of the cells have a face absorbing the warmth of the sun, drinking in the colour yellow. As you see these cells relaxing the whole of your stomach begins to relax, let go and create an experience of warmth, softness and release.

The area of the throat is responsible for all information being digested and expressed. The cells here are bathed in an aqua marine and turquoise. When you feel those colours in that area of your body swallowing becomes easier and more relaxed. Each of the cells are communicating with each other, the sparkle of turquoise allows the flow to be measured and gentle. Hold those colours there and let go of any blockages in communication to others or with yourself.

Feel all these major organs; kidney, liver, lungs and stomach all with cells that are happy to do their job in order to serve you in this body to ultimately discover the treasure. There is a specific cell Meditation on YouTube.

4. Geometry and Mandalas

I am not talking about those boring math classes but the place where art meets science; where all of nature expresses itself in numbers, geometry – the ultimate display of perfection. From the sequence of numbers on petals, to the fractals of shells all mathematically timed and organized. Out of this display of angles, dimensions and patterning comes amazing diagrams known as Mandalas. These are amazingly geometrically apportioned designs with mathematical precision manifesting as an entrancing tool to focus the mind.

Above all, as we look at the architecture of our own inner home; we can see that our own human bodies constitute a geometry and architecture. The golden mean is the equation that is illustrated in a rectangle where two thirds of who we think we are as a human being is always looking to be reconnected to the perceived lost one third or missing piece of us. Often this idea can be demonstrated in woman/man's search for "his true self" or exploring the void. Or expressed another way that part that is always seeking out what it feels is missing! We see this missing aspect in buildings where a corner is not fulfilled, or part of the square or rectangular shape is missing. Is this reflected back to us inside by our environments?

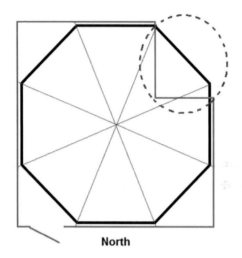

North

I once was offered accommodation and when I went into the room it was totally misshaped. It was neither square nor rectangular and I instinctively declined it. Interestingly I was informed later someone had committed suicide in that very room. So the shapes of places we find ourselves in has to resonate with how we FEEL that place on the inside of us.

If you meditate by just focusing on shapes you become aware of how they feel for you on the internal landscape. Colours are no different. Here is what you do.

Focus on different colours and shapes and spend five minutes and see what happens on the inside. A great exercise to sharpen up your sensitivities and realize how the colour and shape of your environment is influencing you on how you feel within. Once again, this then in turn affects the vibrations that you are exuding.

7 Days To Transform Your Life

All architecture has building blocks of shapes from arches, to squares, rectangles and triangles. Meditating on shapes gives you a different expression internally. Gaze for 5 minutes on different colours and shapes and register how it impacts you. Colour is also an influencer of your mood, emotions and feelings. Ask each time how is this affecting me and making me feel: Book of Shapes & Colour – access link in index.

These shapes and colour make up hypnotic images such as Mandalas. It is a way of focusing on the centre of something and within that shape all the other shapes and colour have a subtle effect upon your own aura and senses. See Below.

https://www.inspiredtoinspire.co.uk

5. Aroma Notes of Interest

The power of aroma has its own system of vibrational energy. If we look at the olfactory system it's possible to see how smells are related to our emotions and memory. The olfactory nerve in our nose can be traced right back up to the limbic system in our brain. This area is where we process aroma and is equated with emotions and our memories. Think of something that reminds you of the past when you smell it – this is the power of aroma. You can recall it immediately because it conjures up a feeling or an emotion. Because aroma is not one of the senses we intellectualize but more emotionalize we don't often have the vocabulary to describe it which is why we use notes, as in music, to describe the different moods of aroma.

Using these aromas creates a different feeling within. Top notes are aromas that are uplifting. Throughout the meditations and visualizations it is possible for you to create an aroma in your brain; breathe in lemon or lime with basil. Some top note aromas are excellent for clearing your head for focus for business decisions, exams, aiming for goals; basil, rosemary.

Middle notes are the midway and balancing – how about breathing and imagining lavender, geranium and juniper? They are used for functions such as wounds, clearing away negative energies and for sleeping.

And base notes always serve a purpose for calming and relaxing such as sandalwood, vanilla-benzoin, rose and orange blossom. These aromas create a base mood – one that calms the mind. Whether you use these oils in a blend for massage, on a tissue to place on the radiator or in the bath, they have the same mood-enhancing effect.

What can you do?

✓ Almond or grapeseed oil are the base oils in which all essential oils are blended

✓ Blends for relaxing and healing are as follows:

✓ 5 drops of Sandalwood, 3 drops of bergamot, 4 drops of rosewood

✓ 3 drops of Benzoin, 3 drops of geranium, 4 drops of frankincense

✓ 3 drops of Lime, 4 drops of rosewood, 5 drops of frankincense

✓ 3 drops of Neroli, 2 drops of juniper, 3 drops of benzoin

6. LABYRINTH

Where have you been today? Did you walk? Did you go down different roads, a different way to the same destination? The flow of movement externally is where we walk and drive and how we are geared towards walking to certain areas, which then create a pattern. We walk in lines, circles, and often square shapes. Our cities, towns and buildings influence us by creating those patterns lived over a lifetime. Think of the patterns you create daily when you go to a place of work or when you do your shopping.

When you are driving you are reading the signs on the way to your destination. We all know the feeling when the lights keep going on red; it feels like there is no flow. This is how we feel in our life, stopping, starting, and stopping.

Movement, metaphorically speaking, featured in the Greek Tale of King Minos and the Minotaur- threading his way back within to find the treasure; the yellow brick road offered a winding long road back to where the magic occurred otherwise known as home and within; all roads lead to the centre. Mazes were all about how we twist and turn in life to get to that place deep within us where we feel at home and at peace.

The power of ritual involves movement and is based on our inner ear function which determines our orientation and proprioception. Psychologically we are being led by large supermarkets and malls subliminally being fed where to go for the milk and bread. The basics more often are found right at the back of the shop; we are indulged in the sense of aroma when at the front entrance greeted by the flowers and bouquets; so movement is also determined by the aroma, they guide us around the shop in a half circle shape but keep us drilled in regimentation of lines.

7 Days To Transform Your Life

If you travel to an Arabic country or Europe the roads have angles, nooks and crannies offering a sense of curiosity as to what is around the corner. In the more modern worlds such as the USA, Australia, much of it has been built on the grid system with its straight road and squares – this elicits a different kind of energy from within you.

But have you ever thought about creating movements and patterns or rituals that serve you? This is the kind of symmetry that supports and creates balance for you.

Think about how you walk in and around your home or where you work. Ask yourself is there something impeding the flow such as a sofa, a desk, a bag of rubbish? You know when you flow through your home there should be nothing that suddenly halts your movement. Maybe you have a focal point in your own home where you offer your intentions of the day, or the gratitude's of your life. Do you have a ritual that focuses your blessings, intentions, attitudes and gratitude's? You can use the incense or carbon blocks, essential oils for the day, crystals for intentions, visualizations, and mantras at your own altar of life.

Movement is created on the outside by elaborate shapes and patterns through choreography and through the shapes created in the asanas of yoga. We have the steps of tai chi and the martial arts that create patterns of defense and attack in movement much like on a chessboard.

The curves of the dance, the angles of the yoga postures the straight lines of the swimmer. The internal movement we have is the flow of life itself; the circulation of blood, lymph, the movement of the nutrients, the osmosis process of fluids being filtered and transported like the precision of a Swiss watch like the ebb and flow of the tide.

What you can be in charge of is this flow of your emotions within your own body. Known as emotional freedom technique or tapping you can do small movements of tapping on specific meridian points. These tapping's on the meridians affect emotions and flow of energy in your body whilst affirming a situation or belief in your life and then changing it to a positive one. I have created some videos for those dealing with clutter and space clearing in their homes, workspaces and commercial areas: see YouTube channel. Creating a flow on the inside can create and reflect that flow you want on the outside.

Whilst we talk about movement and how our environments are affecting that shift within we can also look at stillness and how having no movement has its benefits also. So why not try being still just for five minutes and see what you notice; along with the breathing exercises or mantra you can ask yourself how this makes you feel.

What Can You Do

Tapping on the significant points (see diagram) whilst tapping for a specific issue in mind creates a calming and connecting effect both on the inside and outside. **Brad Yates**, in his videos, always begins with a powerful affirmation; **"Take Responsibility for your own wellbeing"**.

Here is an example on how to get started:

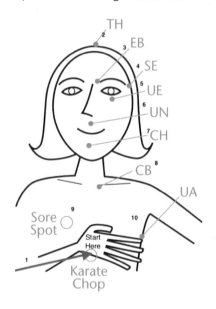

Start off by tapping with your right or left hand, and tap with two fingers on the karate chop site which will be on the other hand. See the statement below that you start with. You have already decided what issue you wish to resolve or let go of. When you have said the statement for a few times you go from the hand-karate chop – to the top of the head. The sequence is below.

The following statement is the kind of thing you say to yourself and continue to tap on the other points above:

Even though _____, I deeply and profoundly accept myself. In the blank area put the problem, issue or anxiety that is troubling you and then tap saying that in the following sequence.

✓ Karate Chop on side of hand of your choice.

✓ Tap on TH – top of the head

✓ Tap on EB – eye brow where indicated

✓ Tap on SE – side of brow

✓ Tap on UE – under eyebrow

✓ Tap on UN – under nose

✓ Tap on CH – chin

✓ Tap on CB – collar bone to the left

✓ Tap on area of sore spot already identified

Tap on UA – underneath arm. Repeat the sequence and you can change whatever it is you are saying. This movement is vibrating through the water of your body and creating patterns that are preferable and positive.

7 Days To Transform Your Life

If you are dealing with issues of clutter, shifting vibrations within the home then I have created some tapping videos exactly for the issue of clutter.

The whole of this day is enabling you to be sensitive to what you feel internally and be aware of how it can alter your perception of your reality. This means discovering more internally, developing a relationship with the world inside, creating visualizations of your own journey in life that allow you to flow and capitalize on the qualities of your own inner structures.

To reiterate taking action (action points and exercises):

INNER FENG SHUI: the internal architecture- THAT IS your mind, emotions, spiritual structures that affects your environments in life.

WHAT CAN YOU DO?

✧ Practice breathing exercise daily – start small amounts just five minutes and extend it as you start to relax into it and see how it transforms your day.

✧ Choose a yoga practice, swimming or a twenty-minute walk that forces you to take deeper breaths once the activity is over you realize how euphoric you feel within.

✧ Disciplining this into your day to some people sounds like a punishment. But when you plan your way to great health and relaxation, the chances of you feeling better in your life are far higher than if you do not take responsibility for yourself. Slippage on not taking care of yourself backs up one day into a big knot that has to be unpicked.

✧ VISUALISATION - try out some of the visualizations on my YouTube channel Cathi Hargaden?

✧ HEALING COLOUR- wear different colours; challenge yourself by wearing colours you have never worn before. Surround yourself in the environment with colours you have never used.

Orange is for self-esteem and poor appetite,

Turquoise for problems with the throat and communicating and saying the truth and being honest with yourself,

Green for health and nature and ancestry,

Red for dynamism, passion, love, getting things done,

Yellow for being present and concentrating and focus,

Blue-lapis lazuli for holding emotion also associated with making & holding money.

✧ AROMA – try this blend for soothing relaxation;

5 drops of sandalwood, 4 drops frankincense, 3 drops lime,

✧ MANTRA – try out this mantra to say each day after the breathing

LOM CEE slowly and clearly.

✧ MOVEMENT-challenge yourself to a totally different set of patterns and movements and see how it affects you. For example take the journey to work on a different route, go to a different place to shop, walk a different way with your dog, do some exercise before you leave home, stretches, take up yoga or swimming.

✧ MANDALA – focus on some of the patterns provided and see how it makes you feel.

✧ ASSISTANCE - over the years of teaching I found people still get stuck in the process even though they know what to do. I would offer assistance if it means getting a result. Go here for free webinars or personal consultations:
www.wealthyspaces.com

DAY 4 – THE FIVE ENERGIES

Day 3 is leading up to today. Through all the different exercises from the previous day you will notice that all energy is coming from within and is connected to a larger energetic universal web. What we have just completed is Feng Shui ing your energy from within. When you start to change your perceptions through the various exercises provided, what you did not see before is now right in front of you. You are picking up on opportunities and ideas from yourself, connecting with people before you never knew, viewing old situations differently and reading the landscape in such a different way that you can only see abundance, opportunity and dynamism all around you.

When you look through a new pair of eyes your perspective of everything around you changes. You see things differently from what you saw before, as one shape is now something else. Could you have been mistaken? Did you misread the landscape? Have your powers of interpretation been miscalculated?

No. When you have a different lens in which to look through, what is before you is interpreted differently. Now the lens you are looking through has created a balance in the space. There are opportunities and messages in that space supporting your creativity and development. The next stage is to introduce the five elements of metal, water, fire, wood and earth, which are five different kinds of energy. When all these elements are present you will feel the difference in your surroundings.

I realize that sometimes we have to go beyond balance in our lives to achieve some great feat, or progress a certain way but ultimately even our own bodies have to return to balance. I like the definition –balance is about harmony and proportion. It is a great place to return to and where else would you be able to find that other than your own business or home. Who wouldn't like a good bank balance, balanced lifestyle, mental health balance even societies when they politically/economically reach the "tipping point" they have to restore some kind of balance to survive.

The idea of balance and change within the Chinese system of Feng Shui has a strong symbolic presence. It acknowledges the different kinds of energy within us as personalities as well as all around us in environments. Think about the people you know who are very grounded like the EARTH, or the person who is very adaptable and flexible like TREES/WOOD, or someone you know who mentally analyses, or is creative, they use the mind to do so and, just like METAL can be melted to create anything but it is sharp to cut things down too. Or the family member who is dynamic and active and full of passion like FIRE, and, of course the WATER person who flows and sinks to depths within themselves but can also flow superficially on the surface too as they are the emotional beings.

We see these elements in the people around us but also these energies are represented through colour, shape, aroma, texture, and movement in our spaces; all that we can recognize through our senses to make sense of our worlds.

5 ELEMENTAL CYCLE

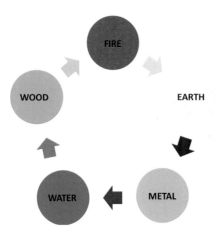

What do these five energies have to do with your home, business or any space?

When you have a balance of each of these five energies represented symbolically or physically that is what creates the magic feeling for people. A feeling of being elevated, grounded, flowing, supported and creative. This knowledge creates your own alchemy of balance, success and freedom.

7 Days To Transform Your Life

Your inner mind is resonating with your surroundings — your space is the product of the seeds you planted. Your space whether it is retail or home is like a garden. It takes less than a minute for people in a room when one starts yawning, everyone starts yawning. Energy is calibrating and infectious. What you start to create in your space starts to influence everything and everyone else. What shows up for you, around you, becomes you.

Have you found paying attention to just one focus or area of your life is often to the detriment of everything else? I constantly see this – the focus – often is either just on work and people then become addicted to their work or their lives become defined by their work. Health is often compromised at the price of other commitments. We all have to make choices and decisions about what is the priority. There's no time carved out for some peace away from the mayhem of a busy life. Even if you deem yourself not to be too busy when is there a time when you experience pure silence, peace, tranquility and a place where there are no demands and you just catch up with yourself?

How do we attain that balance in the different areas from work, financial balance, creativity, family, health and relationships, and support networks? Sometimes one or more of those areas are neglected and that can then become the big pain. A balanced life allows a feeling of harmony so that most, if not all, the different areas of our life are being maintained or heard.

But, within us all, there lies an oasis of peace and calm. Out of all the chaos on the outside who wouldn't want to create that place of balance? All these pains of being on a hamster wheel; all this viewing of the circus on the outside being pulled in and deluged by the noise. Is it not time to get off the carousal and create your own space of harmony and peace – is that not what really matters? When you give these moments to yourself it then ripples out to all around you including the wider spaces in which you reside.

As an occupational therapist, I see people who have devoted their time to habits which were destructive to themselves and others – their lives become out of balance and now they are taking drugs and alcohol to cover up the grim reality of their lives. Others have spent their time on work and then neglected their health and so are now chasing up the years of not exercising or eating properly. We are responsible individually for that balance and sooner or later it does catch us up.

Is this imbalance something we want to feel inside? Or is peace and harmony and calm a better option? One of the best reminders or signs is to place that harmony and balance in and around your space.

What is Inside of You is Around You

This statement is true of the five elements; whether symbolic or real, having a balance is what creates ease. When you have **dis**-ease you have no balance.

The ancient five elemental system besides being used in Feng Shui is also integral to many other systems like acupuncture, shiatsu and herbalism. Many years ago I worked with the elements in relation to massage. It is possible to have a massage that earths you, or one that creates a feeling of flowing water or being pulled and extended as though a branch on a tree, or a metal massage which is a form of just holding the head and containing the stimulation of the mind

To reiterate, the ancient system of the 'I Ching' is all about change and creating a balance and managing that change is paramount. It is no different for our feelings and the organs within us. The human being is constantly trying to balance

himself within but some people just get used to living in patterns that have no balance at all. When I say balance I am talking about the five energies of wood, earth, metal, fire and water.

At first you might think is she nuts? I don't have these things inside of me but once again they are representations/ symbols to explain our feelings that are difficult to articulate. Each organ has a different function but they are associated with different emotions. This has been written about for centuries, I am making the connection between the elements or energies on the outside and how they resonate within you.

• The element of **wood**- how much flexibility and adaptability is there in you? -areas of the liver and gallbladder associated with emotions of anger, shock, rage are often repressed deep within the body.

• The element of **earth**- how grounded are you? areas of the stomach and large intestine, deep sadness and melancholy, but also the area for sympathy, nurturing and caring.

• The element of **water** – how deep are your emotions, which are associated with fear and anxiety and represented in the water organs of the bladder and kidneys.

• The element of **fire** how much joy/laughter and activity is in your life? It is associated with the heart and small intestine.

- The element of **metal** is your thoughts creating both positive and negative ideas; whatever we sow we reap associated with lungs, skin and large intestine. Often what we are thinking can manifest in how we breathe, what shows up on the skin and the inability to digest food. The metal element, our thought patterns, can create grief and sadness if there is no balance in the thoughts.

We need a balance of the above in order to function optimally. Each person's needs are different and each element will undoubtedly operate differently because we are all unique. That is why when you meditate using the breathing techniques in the previous day, you begin to realize what your needs are. You begin to realize that you have a shortage of **earth**- you are not grounded sufficiently, perhaps you are blocked so there isn't enough flow in your life- **water** element; or you have too much flexibility in the **wood** for other peoples' needs but nothing for your own then you need some more back bone to your tree strength which needs to be controlled. Our everyday language at all times uses the language of the five elements; go with the flow, bending like a tree, floating on the stock market full of fire in the belly; and being earthed!!

It is these same five elements that we will also code into your own space so you understand where is the earth to ground yourself, what do you place in your space to symbolize the flow of water, how to express growth through the wood element and why having a bit of each of these elements will make any space you live or work in feel balanced.

The five elements are also symbolic in understanding ideas, actions, processes and intricate thought patterns. They can be used as metaphors on how we process anything in our lives from the beginning of a great idea to the completion and final manifestation of that idea; such as how to start a business. See webinar on Business at http://www.wealthyspaces.com

We could even use the five elements in relation to sounds, or aromas. Words and aromas have vibrations from low to high and each of them resonate with the five elements. For the aromas you would have **wood**- sandalwood, **fire**-cinnamon, **earth**-frankincense, **metal**-rosemary, and **water** – lavender.

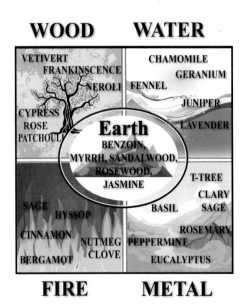

7 Days To Transform Your Life

As **T Harv Eker** in his many lessons reiterates, if you don't feed yourself and don't look after your own roots then no fruits can bear of the tree.

That tree is you!

You are the tree and in order to grow healthily, you need all the resources, just like the tree. Without one of those five elements the other four are running on empty. So think of it in terms of nutrition. You need the vitamins and minerals that is the metal element from the soil, the water you drink, enough vitamin D from the sun which is the fire element and enough green chlorophyll to facilitate your growth in the wood.

When people look for some secret formula or code to success they often look outside of themselves for that fulfillment. However, the secret code lies within you. Combined with the exercises yesterday and the vision board tomorrow we look at how to get the information within you, decode it and display it on the outside in your environment, so you are following YOUR path not what is scripted by others! This will come together on Day 5, and Day 6.

THE PROCESS OF THE FIVE ENERGIES OF LIFE

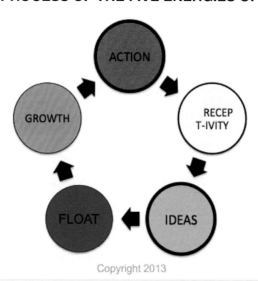

The five elements are also a representation or a metaphor of a process of absolutely anything you wish to accomplish. But each individual element has a personality or flavour of its own. We, like the elements, are individuals, but in our totality, like the cycle above, we create a culture, a community, a civilization and a society.

Using this natural cycle, we see that the minerals in the soil and all the precious compounds are transported by water whether it is rivers, rain, or oceans. The water also feeds the trees and the world's forests. Without it there would be nothing. The forests and the trees are chopped down and used for fuel or to clear a space. Inadvertently forests are destroyed because of fire through the heat of the sun or deliberately destroyed by humans out of destruction or to clear a space.

When all the fires are out we are left with the burnt embers, all reduced to earth again. It is within the earth we once again discover the precious stones, minerals and fossils, and the cycle begins again. If we do not have all these five elements or energies in our life we can feel imbalanced or basically burnt out.

We can compare this cycle or metaphor to our own internal energies. Metal is the mind because the mind cuts ideas. It glimmers like gold with its brilliant ideas and it eradicates like a scythe when something is no longer needed. It is through our minds that we hold our ideas and we float them in water by discussing or ruminating over in our minds and then we go this way or that just like a river flows. The water element denotes feeding and watering our ideas. The wood element, with the assistance of water helps to grow those ideas. Then our business or our life begins to branch out into other areas of growth.

Our ideas are fully developed when we bring energy and light in the form of the Fire element. We have grown them to full fruition. We act out those ideas through the element of Fire. We take Action. The results of those ideas are then earthed and we see the fruits of our efforts. Grounding our accomplishments results in what we have done with the energy we used in that cycle. Whether it is through a job, business, or other endeavor we welcome the fruits of all energy consumed. All wealth is a form of energy. Money is a form of wealth. Money is just one of the currencies, which holds our energetic value. What we consume our time on in earning a living gives us a value. The value of that time or action spent is manifested as money. What we do with that money or energy can create even more by reinvesting or it can stagnate, or just be enjoyed or lost.

Whatever the outcomes of our own cycles we find ourselves creating new ideas with different branches and manifesting new results. And the whole cycle is repeated again. We never end up in the same place because whilst these cycles are akin to nature and its seasons we live in spirals. The spirals are either going up or down. When we return to the beginning of a new cycle we are in a different place.

This cycle can be used for anything you want to achieve in your life. When it comes to setting up that balance with messages of harmony/business/inspiration in your home you want to know what is it going to look and feel like to those who reside in that space.

On Day 6 you will be shown how to place each element within your space. When you do this you are activating the energy that is associated with each of the elements and feelings. They then in turn are reflecting back to you YOUR MESSAGE.

To summarize; you have been introduced to the five elements or five energies that are in the universe. We have used these energies to create a balance. They enable a good flow of energy or chi to flow in and around all spaces. These five energies are important because they support our creativity, our aspirations including health, wealth and relationships.

It is an opportunity to express yourself and transfer what lies between your two ears onto the four walls that surround you daily. This is called taking control of YOUR environment and placing there what you want to hear, feel, see and smell so that it helps you radiate your own dynamism and balance. It also enables you to reflect back a message that YOU want to hear and to perceive in a way that is empowering you. There is no need to listen to messages that have been designed or programmed through many channels like the radio, TV or computer.

In the meantime, become familiar with what the five energies look like and do the following exercises:

This exercise allows you to develop your senses. At first it may be difficult to distinguish but it fine-tunes both the inner and outer environment allowing you to discover the energies that exist all around you!

Look-feel-smell around in your own space and identify the five elements whether colours, textures, aroma or shape.

EXAMPLES

- Fire colours – red, pink, maroon, dark ember. Objects that have a triangular point or flame, anything that associates with warmth or heat. Pictures of animals like lion, tiger, elephant they are fire energy. Aromas of spice, heat and warmth like mandarin, cinnamon, clove, orange.

- Earth colours – yellow, brown, terracotta, orange. Objects made from earth, hessian, ceramics or square shape. Aromas of rosewood, sandalwood, patchouli, benzoin.

- Water colours– blue, aqua, turquoise, water features, pictures depicting water. Aromas of geranium, fennel, lavender.

- Wood colours – green, teal, lime, anything made from wood, pictures depicting fields, forests and Nature. Aromas of cedarwood, cypress.

- Metal colours – silver, gold, copper, steel, crystals, pictures denoting strength of metal like bridges, trains, cars, and information technology. Aromas of sage, basil, rosemary, bergamot.

- Notice which is predominant i.e. plenty of metal and is there a lack of wood? Maybe no plants. Too much fire but no water?

Taking action Awareness Exercise:

This is an exercise for you to position yourself in certain places in order for you to SENSE what it is you pick up from the following:

- Choose a mirror on your wall that you look into frequently, for one week take the mirror away and notice what happens.

- Sit with nothing around you at all but emptiness.

- Sit placed in a corner facing it.

- In front of a plant

- Top of stairs

- Bottom of stairs

- In front of electrical equipment, place all the computers, photocopiers, devices around you

- In front of an open window

- In front of a desk/chair

DAY 5 – GOING WITH THE FLOW ON YOUR FENG SHUI VISION BOARD

We all love stories whether children or adults. They take us to another place using the tools of our own imaginations through colour, tone and design. Children create their own fantasies of bringing in people and places into their make-believe world almost as though there is no bridge between what they see and feel around them and how their inner lives resonate.

What story would you like to be able to tell yourself and what would it look like? What are the seeds you are germinating today for the life you wish to live?

I have a lot of stories to retell. For example, when I was a radio journalist out in war-torn Nicaragua in the 1980s, I found myself in the hills at a community radio station. Guns were going off in the background but I got back to the main station safely. The station manager of Radio Insurrection sent me back to the capital city with a soldier driving in a Land Rover through a terrible rainstorm. I saw the red soil rivers flow down the roads.

Conjure up an image and you are almost there yourself.

7 Days To Transform Your Life

These are all stories but their seeds were sown a long time before I got there. Through music and internal pictures I yearned for foreign cultures and environments. Something took me away from my existing environment that was less than stimulating.

In the previous day you cleared the clutter around you and inside of you for a reason. Day 5 is about being clear and focused on how you would like your life to be, how it would feel and what it looks like. Today is an opportunity to start afresh and start creating the vision you want to step into.

The previous day with the five elements are part of the jigsaw and today we are focusing on creating that vision on a board with NO LIMITATIONS on your dreams and aspirations. You can express your dreams beyond the perimeter of the board. Ensure you can still see what the message is, then it can go on a wall.

How YOU design this picture of feelings, visuals, and sounds will be reflected in your own personal transformation. How to create that life for yourself on the inside is going to be directly reflected back to you on the outside. That is why it is important to ask yourself and keep on asking yourself, "What Do I want"?

No matter how imaginary your picture seems or feels, pictures, words and colours have a vibration that elevate you to a place you want to resonate inside and out.

Here are some ideas to get you started on creating that image and feeling.

- What colours would you want to have in your picture; blues greens or yellow oranges?

- What are the landscapes, people, nature, activities, spaces you would want to create for yourself

- Political and social distractions will always be there. The chaos of the planet is always there and the only way to change that planet at all is to change YOU! All ripples of energy come from you. So ensure your Feng Shui Vision Board is dynamic and focused. Clarity is wealth.

Remember what is around you is within you and that is true of what you choose to place on your Feng Shui vision board. I have yet another story.

I went to Canada many years ago to look at properties north of Toronto. The scenery and ambience were breathtaking; beautiful green scenery, forests, lakes and trees surrounded an amazing maple tree house. I came to a decision on one final house. It had its own theatre, sauna-steam room, and a beautiful bathroom with an acre of land around it. Whilst I made an offer it was not accepted but what happened when I returned home was amazing. My boyfriend, after being back a few days, expressed surprise. He pointed out that there on the wall of my home – was an identical house to the one I had seen in Canada. The entrance, shape, design everything! I began to realize the magic of showing up, intention and subliminal messages we can establish for ourselves and the life specifically we want to lead within the last bastion of our own power – that is our four walls and between our two ears.

So today I am going to show you what you need and how to get started. The difference between the Feng Shui vision board and an ordinary vision board is the former follows a pattern pertinent to the nature of numbers and energy flow. When we do this Feng Shui vision board it is using a system that is associated with the ancient Chinese Lo Shu Square. It is a focus on the five elements, there is a process and I am guiding you in accordance with that flow. I will be guiding you on the nine aspects of your life from relaxation, meditation to wealth, health, relationships, accomplishments and focusing on where you want your own personal life to flow.

Having gone through a western world's education system I saw no guidance towards this focus, intention or creativity of energy at all. No system to hang your dreams onto, no place to entice out what makes you passionate and alive, no delivery or invitation to contemplate the bigger aspects of your life. There were no discussions on how can I add and deliver value to other people and what would it look like. Nothing to suggest that I could be something other than what has been defined by where I live and who my family are.

Therefore, this is a great exercise for young children to participate in. It is not a race to the top but this exercise allows them to align their energy flow in a way that supports their desires, passions and creativity. As Paul Santisi says, **"When you are lined up and dialed in you are ready to go"**.

In this exercise the following are required:

- A cork noticeboard – size is up to you – I often carry mine around from various places so mine is 2.5 feet by 1.5 foot.

- Marker pen

- Access to internet/magazines/photos

Please note that this board is for your own private perusal. One thing I have learnt is when something has not yet manifested and is still in the fertilizing process or in vitro it loses some of its magic and energy when made public. How great is it when you have your own secret on a board that you created and choose to visualize. There is something fun about it and is the entrance to your own inner values and worlds of dreams.

Based on the elements I taught you in the previous day now we will use the elements: Earth, Water, Fire, Metal and Wood in the nine areas of your life onto the board.

Ultimately, this vision is in preparation for the design for your home.

The question you want to ask yourself now is

What Do I Want My Story To be About?

Divide the board into nine squares. Each will represent an element such as fire, earth, water, metal and wood.

Each square represents an aspect of your life. What you put on the board in that square is what you intend to create in your own life.

The only variation in this story is if you decide to create a family board where everyone is part of the creative process. This is a great way to get everyone cooperating in a group image but failing that, do one for yourself.

Using a corkboard will allow you to hang things on it, such as a crystal in a bag or a sack of gold coins.

The sequence of the nine squares follows an ancient pattern of energy flow. It is a process that goes from fertilizing a seed of thought to creation and ultimate manifestation. The shape that the flow creates is the symbol of Saturn, the planet that teaches us life lessons. Rather than resist it why not jump on board and enjoy the journey as you are about to discover!

BLACK SQUARE 1

Let's start with square no 1, which is in black and has to do with the water element and where your journey is going to start flowing towards. Photos, pictures or anything you put here denotes where you want to flow in your life. Are you flowing towards the kind of house or country you would like to reside? Is it an achievement in education, a business you want to create? A family – a spiritual state? Here put a picture of how that would look, anything that indicates a feeling of joy, peace, contentment. Remember my picture of the house in Canada? The black box has to do with water so make sure you have that element in any picture to denote the energy of flow. You have to define your own feelings, images as though you already have them.

Wallace Wattles, in his book **"The Science of Getting Rich"**, emphasizes holding that image in your mind's eye. This exercise is ideal for holding that image. You do not even have to be looking at it. Hung up, it is subliminally affecting you through its shape, colour and design. In the exact same way the TV monitor is on in a part of your room – you may not be watching it but the presence of it is constantly there. This is how the marketing and advertising business works enticing you to **feel** their product and once you have seen it 5000 times through the power of repetition it becomes a part of what you are used to seeing and having around you. It becomes the norm- it becomes your life! It becomes You!

It is like branding a business. You know when you see the big Yellow M anywhere in the world – it means eating junk and business!! Kerching! The same for your board. Make the pictures speak to you, get the messages up there. You need to be telling yourself, even yelling at yourself, because your story is everyone's story. The energy from that board is the energy served up in the world. That is how you change the world. That is how you change YOU! That is how you TRANSFORM your life! The vibrations you create for yourself ripple out to your community, to the culture, and to the world. Yes, it all starts with one emotional thought form and ripples like a pebble thrown into a lake.

PINK BOX 2

The area of the pink box has to do with special love and relationships in your life. One particular person here could be illustrated in a real photo or the kind of person you are looking for. For couples, you can have a special picture together and continue to rekindle the feelings that brought you together in the first place. This is one of the earth boxes so it is putting down a foundation for something in the realm of emotions, feelings and love to be built upon. It is not going to be instant. Remember the five elements – everything is a process or a system!

What is the nature of true love – how does that feel and look like? You must decide, not some media mogul! Once again put your own photos next to someone you would like to spend time with or the qualities of that person. If you cannot find someone, create something that conjures up or symbolizes those feelings and pictures.

Textures of velvet, lace, satin and silk-colours of love-pink, red, maroon, and crimson. Choose to use symbols of two, passion, love, romantic places and travelling with a special companion. You could create your own love poem or story placing it in a pink envelope here. Use the power of your own creativity to create the life you want.

GREEN BOX 3

This area is for your health, ancestors and family. The wood element is like the foundations of your health and the hereditary of your very being. Your health can be dictated by your genetics, although environments also influence your quality of health. Here you can have pictures of good health, taking care of yourself, beauty spas, and retreats to retire to for keeping a balance in your life.

In this box place photographs of the family, or a healing garden, anything that creates a better mental and physical health for yourself. Pictures of bowls of fruit, or a health plan. Take photographs of yourself doing Yoga, Pilates, walks and nature landscapes or inspirational pictures of what you would like to achieve. As we are all individuals what is important to you is not as important to me, which is why this board is highly personalized. Your family might be a group of friends, grandparents, foster parents or anyone who supports you emotionally and practically. Who are the healthy companions, friendships networks you wish to attract into your life-get a visual that represents that and place it in this box. People are part of your environment and we know that who you hang around with will determine that quality of your life. Entice the best energies of trust and integrity that you value into this space.

The flow of the elements - water, earth - flow with your ideas, your photos, and your proclamation to yourself that this is what can be created. This box is the wood element that is growing fast. It is that initial blast of great energy reaching for the sky and if you can epitomize that idea it will reflect that energy back to you from the board.

CRIMSON BOX 4

This is the box of a mature wood element. That means your ideas are growing into something that is identifiable and perhaps tangible. How lucky a person are you? This is a box of good fortune attracting the riches of the world- whatever you deem them to be. This is about attracting luck to your door in whatever guise. But you have to prepare yourself to feel lucky because luck only attracts more luck. People who say they are not lucky do not realize how lucky they are. In the bigger scheme of things, the person next door is often more worse off. What is luck? According to the Roman philosopher, **Seneca "Luck is what happens when preparation meets opportunity"**. This vision board is about getting prepared and aligning your good energy so it is synchronizing with the attraction of opportunity.

A story like this will demonstrate the principle. I had a paediatric health condition, which later in life caused me problems walking. I ended up in hospital on traction for two months-a bit of a guinea pig because they had not seen it before in a female in her twenties. Now, I did not know how this was all going to work out for me. I was a swimmer and a sprinter and did not know if I would walk again.

7 Days To Transform Your Life

Was I unlucky that they had not noticed it earlier? Who knows! I was forced into a period of reflection; given the opportunity to get off the carousel of Life. This period actually prepared me for the experiences in my life to follow. A long period of reflection, being still and being forced to take responsibility for my own health created a different kind of thinking. I became more conscious of healthy eating and exercise, meditation and how environments affected me. In the years to follow I had my own health show on a community radio station, I taught complementary health, meditation, and Feng Shui. A health professional career gave me the best training in Feng Shui (noticing the grimness of many hospitals) and having access to over 2000 homes and offices. I also travelled extensively because being forced into a hospital bed not knowing the outcome was great preparation to get out there and live life fully! I am not saying you want to be forced into a period of ill health in order to prepare for anything. If you are aware you can start those preparations now on your vision board so when opportunities come along you are aligned to act upon them.

The more thankful you are for the luck you have now only opens up more space to receive more. So good fortune to you is what? Gold, silver, money, opportunities for expression, great friendship network, writing a book and its success, great family. Remember, this is your story. Both receiving and giving create that yin yang balance I have been talking about. Receptivity and giving are a balance.

YELLOW BOX 5

Turning and turning in the widening gyre The falcon cannot hear the falconer; Things fall apart; the centre cannot hold;

W. B. Yeats

The centre is the command area of your ship. All responsibilities return to you. If you don't take to the helm of your own ship others will do so. In this area you want ideas and Images of balance, wheels of fortune and stillness in this earth element. If you are not **still** enough you cannot see the board around you and what you have created for yourself. If you are always moving and racing ahead when do you catch up to reflect and take in what is important to you?

For anyone who knows the game of chess, rash, impromptu moves are not going to bring you what you want. But yes, you still have to move.

Anything in this square that allows you to be the emperor or empress – the command of your ship – the king or queen of your kingdom – that is you! You influence all the other areas of your life from this command point, be specific on what each box means for you in your life.

Remember, this is YOUR story. What do you want to be in command of and how do you want to see yourself?

This Earth element is the most important box of all – it is the strongest box and the seat of ultimate power in your life and on the board, so what you put here is crucial. It could be anything – a clock for time, a prayer for the journey, and the symbol of balance, heart of Love as the central theme. Maybe there is just one focus on your life at the moment put a symbol in the central yellow box. Justice, wisdom, integrity and/or guidance—these are all values and qualities that you may wish to exude in the execution of all the other areas in your life.

GREY BOX 6

This is the metal element – the energy known for its military precision in thinking and in activating its strategy. Grey is part of the corporate world, especially computers and I.T. This is the area for travel and business. The technology now allows businesses to go global.

Ask yourself, what is the focus here for me? Is it a vision of a specific business or a particular vocational career? A service you want to provide? Does that business involve travel? How you deliver the information of what you offer and how it is valued would in some way be illustrated in this box. Your vision here wants to be very clear how you want to feel or who you want to become in your job, business, or any other roles you undertake in life.

Images of travelling would represent how you might want to go global with your business or what you offer of value internationally. Pictures of technological images, courses to enhance your knowledge would also be pinned here.

It is your story and you decide by placing symbols and pictures that calibrate the very energy you want to draw into your life in this area.

WHITE BOX 7

This box is a softer metal energy. Nothing like the grey box which is about a mathematical laser-edged focus on business and problem solving. This is a softer metal energy almost mercurial, like silver and gold moving in liquid form. This box represents a feeling when your ship has come into dock with the results of your efforts. This space is for relaxation, travel and enjoying the fruits of all your hard work and learning with people around you who you treasure.

Where would you like to see yourself relaxing – city or countryside – another country? And whom would you choose to be spending that time with? Maybe you choose a cruise or whatever creates a feeling of letting go.

This is the box of your own creative talents, so only you can decide what would you like to create; a family, a house, or maybe a ship. Maybe you want to look for alternative ways of living? This is your box of the future so whilst you relax you let go and just BE. This area you place pictures of what you wish to enjoy or create for your future.

LILAC BOX 8

In this box you create the image of focusing within yourself. The place from whence all your energy is sourced. If you do not create a place or a time for yourself then when and where will you ever have space to reflect, create and ponder on the bigger curiosities of life?

Picture a place you would like to retreat to. There are many amazing images of Indian ashrams, Ayurveda centres, and exotic retreats in Bali, Australia, Malaysia, Canada, and Costa Rica. It's important to have an environment for you to get away from everybody as it is inevitable you will require recharging your batteries no matter what kind of life you lead. Focus on the big picture, but create your own retreat at home too.

This is the earth element area associated with your deeper beliefs in the world. Your philosophy and anything you want to symbolize on your board that has an esoteric or mystical concept can be expressed in this area. You can write a mantra, or a poem from a respected writer, motivator or yourself.

It is your box. It is your faith, belief and philosophy that expresses the nature of the balanced lifestyle you prefer to draw towards you. Represent that in this box through pictures, photos and words.

RED BOX 9

The Fire element is the ultimate pinnacle of energetic passion and dynamism, which often occurs in a cycle of energy. This is your very own **shine** moment! Your thoughts, strategy, work, ideas, communication, transactions, and belief systems come to fruition. This is the area to illustrate and demonstrate the ultimate achievements that you have developed and created for yourself. This is where you visualize what you want to be good at and known for- from a good mark at school to a medallion for swimming. These are just examples.

What does that look like? You can fill the box with anything; school awards to mementos from countries you've traveled to or even family reunions. The board really is your OYSTER!

One thing is for sure-this whole exercise is a great way of pulling out of you your dreams and aspirations and getting you to become laser sharp on what they would look like, feel and resonate. You could even take one look at the board and commit to your memory – keep it in your thoughts throughout the day.

I know this is scary at times. Humans often want to remain limited, be confined or defined by their peers, families, and politicians. But you have the capacity to go beyond anything where you are now located whether that be how you feel within or what you see around you.

7 Days To Transform Your Life

But first, you have to do the work. I have been in so many environments and even relationships where I realized I dared to dream, but the other person had no dreams or the environment pulled you down for dreaming.

This board is not about reflecting back on your shortcomings or limitations. Often we don't always know what is inside of us until we get an opportunity to illustrate and demonstrate. This is an invitation to be as big, as broad and as preposterous as possible because confidence in your Feng Shui Vision Board is the confidence in you! If you do not prepare now, how will you be ready or aligned to the opportunities that come your way? This is also known as Your Good Luck!

Your symbols will be different from anybody else – this is where your creativity and imagination comes into play. What opportunity do you really ever get to put outside of yourself the idea of your story? Your story is just as important as all those celebrities who people spend hours and hours of their time preoccupied with; what they wear, own, what cosmetic surgery they promote and the endless products all on the back of fame. This is YOUR story you are creating and this requires time spent on you, not on fake and deceptive portrayals of what is deemed success! Your perception is the most prized aspect to guard against. Make sure you are not in servitude to others' perceptions but set up your environment so that you choose to interpret your space in a way it favours and supports you.

Taking action (action points and exercises):

1. Purchase a cork notice board and some pins

2. Using a black pen mark out 9 boxes on the board.

3. Collect pictures, take photos that sum up the energy of what you want to create, find pictures that express your story and then have them printed.

4. Keep your vision board a secret or private. A thin veil of cloth attached to cover if there's a possibility of others viewing it.

5. Fill in the boxes in the order suggested above so your board flows with the energy of the elements.

6. Try not to keep changing the boxes. – Think before you earth your dreams and desires.

DAY 6 – HOW TO CREATE A CODED PLAN OF YOUR HOME AND ROOM

Having explored what lies within the inner house and having created a master board of your own story, it is now time to display changes, superimpose those dreams, aspirations, and resonances and calibrate the feelings into your own home. I am going to show you how.

We hear a lot in personal development about getting focused and creating a vision for your life, even in the chapter on meditation. We were trying to access your inner architecture for all the different rooms of your life: peace, spirituality, finances, love, health and so on. However, how do you manifest and symbolically place around you what you want your story to be about? What is the feeling? Everything is about how you set up your environment so it makes you feel a certain way; maybe elevated, inspirational, motivational, or transcendental.

As an occupational therapist I visited many people in their homes who were dealing with depression. If I asked people to make some changes so that they could feel better it was difficult for them to know what they wanted to change internally. But when I invited clients to look around their environment and ask what would they like to change on the outside they immediately found one thing, no matter how small, that they pointed to.

One client who had been chronically depressed painted his whole room a different colour. In fact he painted it a terracotta colour – the colour of Earth. Being active is often an issue if you're depressed. He took some control over his own environment after we had a discussion on how different colours affect our moods. This change is just one step but it is about getting people to invest themselves in what they surround themselves daily.

This is called transformation!

- You're clearing away what's around you

- You're focusing on what you want to feel, see, hear, and elevate to

- You are putting that in a code into your four walls

- You are living how you want to feel, be, and do!

Everything in life is a code! What do I mean by that? I have already mentioned The Book of Changes and its 64 different situations we can face in life. Likewise, in the game of chess, like life, we are faced with choices and decisions. The whole of creation has a strange random orderliness to it with trees, plants, and shells- all designed to have a certain amount of leaves and petals, and they follow the Fibonacci series of measurement. FIBONACCI series is a repeat of numerical patterns where the measurement of everything runs in a sequence.

0,1,2,3,5,8,13,21,34,55 The previous two numbers make up the next number. Expressed in shape they translate into spirals, petals and this is the intelligence that lies all around us in nature, our spaces and within us.

As humans we often pick up patterns that are going on around us all the time; involving colour, sequences, numbers, shapes. We use these patterns as cues for meaning; our perception of those patterns gives a meaning. That is why what is around you now is a pattern and the question you ask yourself what are the patterns reflecting back to you?

Symbols of power are everywhere! Just look around in the country you live in. There are insignias on buildings, symbols of snakes and tigers on cars, and eagles all denoting wealth, power and control. We have statues and buildings all reflecting back to us who was once in power and who is still in power. Important people occupy such buildings and the rest of the population projects their own power onto those people. Now it is time to create your own code within your own four walls so it reflects back to you precisely what you wanted on your Feng Shui vision board.

7 Days To Transform Your Life

Even for those who are skeptical would it not be better for YOU to put the order into your life rather than it be imposed upon you by the TV, newspapers, the government, the religion or the computers or pictures that surround you now?

That is why the Bagua Grid below using the compass points is a code. You can symbolically use this in your own rooms, homes or work places. This grid will enable you to attain the maximum amount of focus and thereby fulfillment for your life.

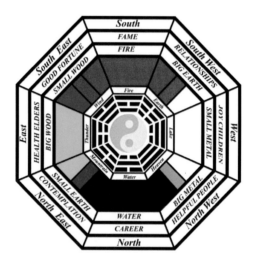

Nobody else has to know – even those who you live with. But I bet you they will be the first to comment on the strange changes and great feelings being "imposed" upon them.

Why not captivate that space by making it work for you to the best of your own progress and development?

Day 6 – How To Create A Coded Plan Of Your Home And Room

This coded template deals with the same nine areas in your life that was on your vision board. They cover good fortune, wealth, health, creativity, spirituality, relationships, self-discovery, and your journey in life. You can choose to focus on one or more areas purely by placing something there that has a meaning and a reflection back to you.

But before we embark on this process we have to ensure that the other five steps or days have been completed. To start the compass process whilst the corners of your space are still full of clutter would only add more to the confusion and chaos of the message or focus you want to create for yourself.

These steps of measuring your room or house, getting a direction on where is north, south, east and west are not difficult. I show you **on my Youtube channel** how to go about that in my video. Below are the steps you need to take. You can see from the template that each direction has a command over an area of your life, and has a specific element that dominates it.

The reason for the south being at the top of the compass is that the Chinese honour the South. It is still magnetic north and south but this is how they illustrate their compass.

The code for your life is like painting a huge vision board on your own personal space. We created the Feng Shui vision board yesterday. Now we get to superimpose that in a subtle manner across the whole room and house or living area. The only difference this time is when you have drawn a plan of your space, go to the front door and acquire the compass direction. If you focus on true magnetic north that will give you all the other compass directions within your space. Superimposing the code template below by aligning it with your personal compass directions you can see which areas in your home are related to specific colours, symbols, images, aroma, design, and features.

A plan of your own room, business, or home lies underneath the grid. You can deduce where your south-east area is and what kind of symbols you might consider to represent your own desires. Below is the tool you can overlay on your plan – download and print onto a transparent acetate.

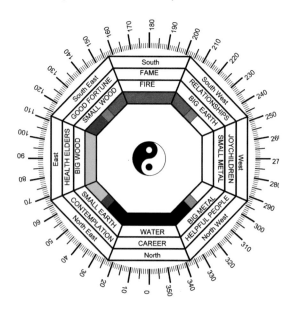

Let's look at the different compass points and understand the qualities, which area of your life it represents and what can you symbolically place there. The compass directions, the elements, and the qualities associated are just symbols of how to organize your space so you are reflecting to yourself a feeling, a mirror of where you are heading, what it looks like and how it feels.

You have to show up for yourself in this world and one way of doing that is showing the value of yourself within your own four walls. What your aspirations are nobody needs to know but when you look around you everything around you supports how you want to feel within.

THE EAST

There is a reason for the wood element, representing your health, being in the east. Like trees, we have an ancestry stretching back hundreds of years. The east is seen as the past. Who knows what our ancestors experienced just for us humans to be alive today. The east represents our past roots whilst the west is our tomorrows.

Therefore, what we place in these areas of our space denotes the qualities of above. You can place people you honour from your past in the east. And, if that is not pertinent then nature is your great ancestor. Place pictures of trees, ancient forest and woodland around the space. The energy of wood, growth, intelligence, expansion relates to qualities that are integral to everyone. You have the support of a past – something that went before you.

The energy of **wood element** is often evident for those who naturally gravitate towards keeping plants around in their space. Plants not only provide our oxygen but they are a reminder of growth. How you take care of your plants is a reminder of how you are taking care of yourself. Failure to water and feed means failure to thrive. The opposite can also occur where we over water and over feed. Often some people can find themselves doing this for others'. Over doing their attention to other people's emotional and physical wellbeing but neglecting their own responsibility for themselves. That is why having plants helps to create that relationship of taking care of yourself as well as something outside of you in a balanced way.

If plants aren't an option, bring in colours in upholstery, curtains or vases of green, emerald, moss, teal, and dark green. Pictures of trees, woodland and forests return us to a very primitive relationship with nature that we almost have forgotten because we are so cut off from it. I know living in the cities this is very true.

Secret Code: Behind your picture place here a green square of silk to indicate health and wellbeing. Or, acquire a plant and place 3 green or blue crystals in the soil. Each crystal denotes a quality, something you want to grow.

THE WEST

The west is represented by the shiny yin metal – it denotes the ability to shimmer, reflect light and offer us potential for the future days. The element of metal is about our ideas. If we think of a metal knife or sword it cuts through the air; it finely cuts and fragments things into smaller pieces. If we think of metal when it is melted it starts to flow and creates a different shape. These are the qualities of our mind. The way we **think** daily means we are constantly cutting things into smaller boxes, ruminating and flowing with ideas. Resistance to change is like the metal that is stubborn and unbreakable - there is a resistance within us. Thoughts that flow are like our great ideas that flow and move onto the next stage in a process. Thoughts that resist become stubborn, obstructive and break.

The west therefore represents the ideas of today for the future of Tomorrow. Once again the theme of preparation, you are preparing your future by aligning with opportunities around you. Those opportunities are the cues that you place in your environment.

The west can be reflected with any kind of crystal from the earth, pictures of what you would invite into your future; anything made from metal and those minerals from the earth; copper, pewter, gold, silver, amethyst, lapis lazuli. Hanging crystals capturing the light of the sun radiate and reflect around the room. When we come into the house and see the rainbow on the walls it affects our mental state positively.

Secret Code: Place a picture here of where you want to go in your future. Frame the picture in anything that is metal.

THE NORTH

Looking to the north – this was considered a fearful area for the Chinese because of historical attacks by the barbarians. The north represents the element of water. Not everybody in the world today gets water from a tap! They have to walk miles to get the water and haul it back. Water is one of the richest commodities in the world and its display is a statement of wealth and riches. If we look at the Far East and some of the European cities, their huge displays of fountains and fish tanks reflect back health, wealth and a life-force. Water has always been synonymous with wealth hence, any display of that in this area of your space will be a reminder of inviting and receiving wealth, psychologically. It can be portrayed in pictures in this area, or the colours of blue and aqua. Plants thrive from the water so also indicative of growth for your good fortune. Where is it you want to flow to? This is a very important area because upon my consultations I discover many people don't know what they want or they are scared to entertain any ideas at all. But once you have grounded a vision, a feeling and it is succinctly depicted it is a constant reminder to the inner workings of your mind that this is the life or way for you! It can be seen on your Feng Shui Vision Board now. Picture your vision you chose on the board. Any features such as a small fountain, or blue, black, aqua glass beads indicate the water element as well as the colours on upholstery or an ornament. Anything that has a wave formation such as curtains trailing with large curves indicates a water movement in the room. When people observe the water colours there is a response of calm, relaxation and letting go of the stress.

Secret Code: Place a gold or silver coin behind a picture. Cannot afford real gold? Place toy gold-as it is all symbolic.

THE SOUTH

The south is honoured because of its red power and vital energy. This area you will consider the colours red, orange, burgundy, maroon and the fire of candles, fireplaces, and pictures of hot summer. In the cycle of the five elements this element is all about taking action in your life. If we look at the seasons it is the summer where we have the utmost energy for action. Whilst metal element is about having the ideas to create something ahead in your life, the fire element is about taking action on those ideas. Pictures that have Ideas such as dancing figures, where there is movement, or sounds and music, which is full of passion. Use aromas that are stimulating such as clove, orange, mandarin, and cinnamon. This is also an area to shine your accolades and for being noticed for all that you do! Pin up your certificates and trophies because the inner glow is now being manifested on the outside with awards, medals and achievements. Yes this is your time to shine!

The ultimate Fire Energy is the human beings inhabiting the space. If you enter the stores in U.K. now there is often a ghostly presence. The lack of human energy, fire energy, reduces the vibrancy of a retail space. Some of the large malls throughout the world, Dubai, USA, Canada there is a deathly silence because there is no life force in these large spaces. The ghostly new built cities of China – all sixty of them – with very few people living, working or doing business casts a presence of lack of energy, lack of wealth. Ultimately the life force is coming from you or your pets!

It is the same for any retail stores, shops, bed and breakfasts and hotels. If the energy has sunk, the guests feel it when they enter. That is why the fire element is also a part of lighting and how it is designed affects us internally. Having people around generates energy for any space in a commercial, residential and retail building.

This spatial arrangement is symbolic. In essence, it's a way of ordering your life so that you reflect back to yourself a balance of how you want to feel and experience your time. You are choosing the cues in and around your environment that remind you what makes you feel great and which way you are flowing.

Secret Code: Place a picture or statue where it is prominent no one needs to know why that light is on that picture or symbol.

Then there are the other four areas of the compass:

THE SOUTHEAST

The south-east is a wood and water area. On a general level it represents growing your good fortune for you and others. This is the kind of wealth that is about your financial health. The wood element is about growth like a tree or a plant. If you don't take care of the roots how can you ever manifest any fruits?

The south-east is about the health of your wealth and how open you are to receiving great fortune. Like nature, the receptivity to the sun and water warrants the survival of the plants. Likewise with people, the power of the mind closes people down often because their own environments are closing them down. There is nothing to elevate, inspire, or motivate. Of course it is a two-way road. The environment inspires but people have their own inner space too in order to inspire and motivate themselves and express that in the environment by making the changes. It is this symbiotic relationship that makes all the difference to peoples' quality of life. Having that vision board in your private space is making a start.

In this area place a demonstration of something you are grateful for because it aligns you for more great opportunities. Symbolically when you water your plants be mindful that you are watering your wealth, health and anything that you would like to breathe life into. You could be watering your health-say this as you do it. Watering your wealth, watering a new attitude or what you want to grow whether business, family or skill. After all this is the very life force in the universe.

Those in confined quarters or limited space can depict these qualities in pictures, aromas and sounds. The colour of money? The smell of money? Wealth attracts more wealth! How often have we heard these idioms in the English language? The colour of money is in the greens, blues, jades, silver and golds. The smell of money is the amber, jasmine, tuberose, mimosa, neroli and frankincense. The sounds of water fountains, fish tanks and plants growing create an ambience of plenty flowing towards you.

Secret Code: Place lapis lazuli blue, turquoise stone onto the base of a money tree or jade underneath the soil of a plant pot – nobody sees them but you are growing your own wealth.

THE NORTHWEST

These areas of the compass all relate to each other. Diagonally opposite south-east is the north-west, the metal strong element of communications, people helping you, business, technology and travel.

Wealth comes from the ideas of metal so relates to the south-east in good fortune. Helping others and communicating in business in the North West opens up the doors to create good fortune for you in the South East. In fact the North West is the business of taking care of you whether that be financially or any other way. When you demonstrate the ability to create wealth from your ideas by helping others it ripples out to communities who need your great ideas. Then you have resources to provide for other opportunities. The very ideas that create a flow of good fortune and wealth are illustrated in the South East.

Here in the North West use your space to denote anything to do with crystal, bright objects that slowly move like a lava lamp. Metallic objects represent the mind. Using hanging crystals with sunlight shining through create an amazing rainbow effect around your walls. What this is doing is introducing creativity into your space. From creativity comes innovation for new ideas related to whatever you are doing in your life whether it be business, organization or voluntary. It also alters and transforms your mood when you walk into your space and see this amazing spectacle of light and colour.

You can introduce copper colours and pewter or anything that shimmers like the ideas of your mind. Pictures that denote communication, connection, people helping others, or travel. What value does your business offer? Is it a service or a product? Is your business offering a solution to a problem or offering value to those who wish to participate in it. Place the spaces, countries you have visited, the landmarks, areas that you are grateful to have seen. Position places you want to visit or those you have already visited which brings a gratitude for more to come.

Secret Code: An atlas or map pinpoints where you want to do business, or visit. Position one symbol that represents the value you would like to offer people. Arrange these symbols so they are connected to anything which has a crystal design; turquoise blue, black, quartz, any of the metals.

THE SOUTHWEST

The southwest part of your space is ordered by the earth element. The kind of earth qualities of this area are about connecting with people. In this area it is about the connection of a partner and building a life with that person. The colours that dominate here are browns, yellow, apricot, and harvest colours. The area, because of the connection to love, will also have some red from the fire element.

Anything that indicates an earth-like quality would be depicted as part of the scene you wish to create in your life. Ceramics, straw, hessian materials-pots and earthenware. Choose pictures that depict the earth and those of a firm grounded relationship. Because it is symbolized by the number 2 – it would be two of something whether that be of animals, humans, or inanimate objects. Remember that it can be depicted all in one single picture the kind of qualities you would like to attract into your life from that significant person.

Secret Code: Use photos of who you would like in your life; consider the nature of their qualities: a poem, message, bouquet of flowers, photo and hide this image only you know it is there.

THE NORTHEAST

The diagonally opposite area is the northeast which focuses on another kind of earth quality known as s p a c e. This space is for receiving, for silence, peace, going inside and reflection. In many ways these two areas interrelate so if you have no space within you then how can you invite anybody towards you? The earth symbols in this area would have terracotta's, yellow, and brown. This area is about your higher beliefs, philosophy and your inner road to your own belief system.

This northeast is about peace, gratitude and humility in your own life. You take charge here of your divine compass no matter what that belief is it is yours to express.

Whether that would be depicted by divine symbols, or the more earth associated systems such as the native Indians, or the Taoist system is purely your own individual choice. If you have nothing of that quality you leave the space free to illustrate whatever you need to go within yourself. Sentiments of gratitude, humility, stillness can be symbolized here.

Secret Code: Leave a pot here totally empty, honouring the concept of space. Or a cup and saucer with nothing in it at all. When you leave a space empty it is an invitation for what you focus on to enter your life.

Good health in the east gives you good prospects for the future, which is the west. Knowing where you want to go depicted in the north allows you to feel great in the south and shine with your trophies and achievements. Space within you allows you to attract the best vibration towards you. And, helpful people, communication and creating new ideas for innovation brings you the good fortune and wealth because you offer value to others in your life.

Once again, you will create the space you have control over and place in it symbols of what you want to attract into your life. Allow it to reflect back to you or remind you that this is your focus and that is what you want.

Many years ago I had a client who was a professional legal worker who had tried to commit suicide. Even though it was his own business he did not want to return to work. During one of his appointments to me, I asked him to describe his office – what was on the wall in front of his desk and behind him.

He said his walls were completely blank. I got him to visualize a picture of why he turned up for work and what was he working for. The picture he had in his mind was one of his family living in a beautiful home. I also got him to think of a picture that would represent strength from behind his seat. For example, behind his desk he could place a picture of a mountain, or a bridge, or strong animal like a lion. Immediately, as though by magic this man began to take some control back into his work/life; he knew exactly what he was going to do. The man walked out of the clinic with a totally different walking gait to that which he walked in. He had a spring in his step walking out and he was in a rush to take back control and design his own life in his space.

This is the power people discover when they realize that their own four walls are their mirror. What they create out there is reflecting back to them. The alternative to not being aware, not changing is regret. If you do not discipline your space to reflect back YOUR dreams, messages and desires then someone else will! The space is about putting in the cues you want to be reminded of in your life. Otherwise, no clarity means no wealth or financial flow.

This spatial arrangement is symbolic. In essence, it's a way of ordering your life so that you reflect back to yourself a balance of how you want to feel and experience your time. You are choosing the cues in and around your environment that remind you what makes you feel great and which way you are flowing.

7 Days To Transform Your Life

Remember to ask yourself the following:

What is my story?

What is the message?

What do I want?

What is my code?

Taking action (action points and exercises)

Identify all the shapes, goods around you that represent the earth element. Do the same for water, metal, wood and fire. Ask yourself what do you need more of? More fire for action, passion, have more water for wealth, finances and flow, more earth for calming, grounding and containment, more wood for growth, progress and health, more metal for creativity, analysis and ideas.

1. **You may have the plans of your home, or you can take the dimensions of your room, or house using the magicplan.app**

2. **I suggest you start with just one room so you get to understand the different compass directions. Then you can place it over your whole space.**

3. **If you have the measurements of your home you can have them drawn by professional plan makers here at a reduced price: www.makingplans.com and quote Cathi**

4. **Once you have your plan, download my template in index onto a transparency; place it over your room by aligning it with your compass points.**

5. **You can take your compass points by going to the front of the house and finding out where is true magnetic north. When you have identified where that is you can place the template and the plan of your home aligning both areas to north.**

6. With the template it will divide your space into eight areas of the compass –defining compass point = area of your life = the main element of that area.

7. Choose two areas of your life you wish to focus on; good fortune and business or journey in life and health. In those areas of your home put in messages, symbols that you wish to resonate. i.e. north = journey = element of water = picture of where you see yourself wanting to go in the following year.

   i.e. south-east = good fortune = wood element = placing a healthy plant, picture of river meandering in valley, or fish tank.

8. Now you understand which element influences which area. Become creative by designing what your message is to be reflected back to you.

9. Once designed. Sit and breathe. Then notice for one week how you respond to your new coded environment.

10. For those who would still like to have assistance in this matter you can contact me for skype calls or consultations:

   http://wealthyspaces.com/product/package-1/

DAY 7 – POWER HUBS OF THE HOUSE

By now you will have cleared the decks from clutter, cleansed the invisible spider webs of emotions and feelings and internally prepared the inner architecture for what you want to see on the outside. On Day 4 we looked at perception changes through the five basic energies of fire, water, earth, metal and wood. Day 5 we then depicted our intentions onto our Feng Shui Vision Board allowing us to code that information into our own homes. In a creative manner we have now superimposed our visions according to the compass directions, elements and our nine aspects of our life. When we look around us, we see our visions and dreams reflected back to us 360 degrees. We are hypnotizing ourselves with the level of energy we wish to encounter rather than submissively accepting a hypnotic box in the corner.

We also have power hubs in our own home. They are focal points, which are like meeting places we repeatedly use to come together, to use a lot of our time, efforts and energy.

From ancient times to today the power of certain points within the earth's crust have special powers and energies. As a result, sacred buildings such as churches and temples were built upon them to capitalize on that special energy. These areas are known as ley lines running throughout the earth and renowned for having buildings built on them in order to attract the best energy. Pagan civilizations honored these areas and thereafter Christianity and other religions would build their sacred sites on them to denote special power.

Buildings, palaces, bridges, and roads are created to bring energies to a place, to attract special vibes. Major buildings like the White House and Buckingham Palace all have a geometric design to harness the energy of the population towards its power hub. All roads lead back to the castle! Windsor Castle! Major decisions and power shifts are made in such locations where people project their energies towards such places. The spas of Europe were the hubs of special healing powers like Biarritz, Bath and Harrogate. The financial magnets attracting people to invest, to make deals in The City **Square** of London, Wall St. and now the bridge leading from China mainland to the island of Hong Kong.

All these hubs of energetic power have pulled people into these spaces because of how it makes them feel whether for health, wealth or success. Whilst these places attract, there are locations that repel.

What do I mean by Power Hubs?

There are specific areas in your home that host the most magnetic and focused energy in the whole of the building. In some homes it does depend on culture. For example, due to light constraints in Zanzibar they use the central atrium for the light of the moon as some people are without electricity.

In warmer countries they may congregate together at the entrance of the home. In the colder countries, it might be in the kitchen, the warmest place of all!

These are the areas to really focus on in your own home – magnets of energy - because they are based on your health, wealth, regeneration and elevation of spirit. Everything around you is aligning up with the feelings and thoughts within. Your perceptions to the reality of your environment interact and make you relate and reflect back.

There are Four Areas: Entrance, Kitchen, Bedroom and You!

1. Entrance

When people arrive at a house that they are going to buy, rent, visit or party in, they have already made a mental and emotional image of expectation. First impressions can always be wrong, of course, but how somewhere looks from afar before even approaching the place is revealing.

As I have frequently expressed and written a book about it:

"Opportunities knock on doors with good vibes" – how many times are people attracted to places because of how they look on the outside from the colour of the door, to the front entrances and the flowers or trees that frame them?

7 Days To Transform Your Life

Be aware of how you approach any entrance whether it is a house, company, or retail unit. It is almost like the entrance is the book cover to a story of the residents. What does your entrance say about you?

What about the kind of key you have to access your home? This key is the gateway to what you have scripted for yourself inside your own cave. From the food stored there, to the aromas, flow and energy of the space inside it will determine your health, wellbeing, mental mindset and balance. Do you struggle to get the key inside the lock? Or are you always struggling to see the lock because of poor lighting due to the darkness. Have you ever wondered why some keys work with ease and others just do not fit? Besides badly cut keys, there is a whole energy that goes with the frustration experienced going through your front door. After the key is fixed, if it continues for some unknown reason it leads to mental frustration fermenting over a long time. The key is important because it accesses your kingdom. And the question is: what are you going to discover when you go inside?

Always keep entrances clean, free from clutter – bins kept away, all greenery or flowers, if they are dead or dying cut them off. Ensure the plants are rounded and have curvaceous leaves as opposed to being pointed in shape and form. If you do have problems with burglary I often suggest herbs of rosemary and sage in pots at the front as they were used during the plague as a form of esoteric protection.

Keep everything alive! Ensure there are lights around the entrance beaming a positive energy as you enter your own home zone. If you have flowers make sure they are bright and fiery. Hanging baskets enlivens an entrance when you invite people into your home. If people have to physically lift their heads up to view it this is excellent. When people elevate their heads it raises the energy within them, leaving them feeling better. Your body has an energy system known as chakras. The circles of energy are situated from your crown chakra through to your throat, heart, stomach and base of spine. When you raise your head you are activating the crown, throat and heart chakra evoking a sensation of awe. Try it!

If anything is broken, or damaged, fix it as it makes it look better. Common sense? Of course it is and yet we all have something broken we are holding onto. Brokenness is a stuck energy. People notice what doesn't work, not what 'works'. Likewise, houses that look broken from the outside have an energy that spirals downwards. You don't want to enter them.

2. COLOUR OF DOORS

Colours are always important at the front entrance. They represent the vibration of the home. This is another invitation to turn over the page and discover who is inside.

Here we see a red and blue door; red to instill the fire, active energy whilst blue is about a wealth energy and can be more official and reserved. Lapis Lazuli Blue is a good colour for business and wealth. In our society, we are surrounded by white, grey and magnolia – they are used a great deal by institutions because they engage the mind and are the color of authority. When we return to our homes the mind is mentally exhausted having related to a workplace surrounded by computers, phones, and magnolia walls.

Be aware of the colour of your door. Put some colour into your life especially when going through the same door daily. Green is the wood element which is about growth like a Tree. Having other colours of flowers around it complements the front entrance you are about to enter.

Wooden varnished doors are a complement to the surroundings and create the image of growth and age. Black doors, like lapis lazuli are more about officialdom or business. Orange and yellow are earth colours, so if you want to feel earthier these are the colours for you. However, in terms of Feng Shui the aim is to allow energy to flow through the entrance and front door with ease which is why black, blue, aqua are colours inviting the water element with the flow of energy into the residence or building.

3. Aromas

How many of us are not only affected by the colours we see, distracted by the clutter of the surroundings of the entrance but are very affected by the aromas we smell?

If it is an unpleasant aroma, we already have made up our minds about the nature of that house. If the aroma is rejuvenating or euphoric, then a trip down memory lane would create quite an effect.

Who doesn't love the smells of rose, sweet pea, wisteria or the herbs of lavender, basil, rosemary, and sage? Of course, if they are associated with bad memories or uncomfortable emotions those aromas are not going to appeal to you.

As subtle as it seems the power of aroma can include a person's feelings pushing them to buy or rent or wanting to return to a specific place..

Aromas have been used in the marketing industry to entice the customer into a shop to buy from coffee and bread to bouquets of flowers. In and around our environments it is really effective to have aromas that rejuvenate, help you concentrate or relax. Imagine as you return home you catch the sweet aroma and how it impacts your emotions hopefully for the better.

I once purchased a concrete boot planter, and inside grew the sweet aromas of blue lobelia and white stock. The aroma was intoxicating especially during the evening- until of course, someone thought it was so alluring that they stole it.

When we see two pots outside the door or two bushes; the colour of the pots and flowers combined are a statement. It's like creating your own brand – what does it say about the people inside? What is the message it is framing? What is the energy of that building?

The colour of the door, the aromas, the overall picture from the kerb- what makes the difference? Chimes, aromas, living matter, colours of the flowers, sounds of the bell or the knocker and a welcome mat.

That's it! When you create or get what I am saying, how your entrance appears is crucial to how you feel when you leave and return to your home. It makes a difference to the people who also arrive at the door as to how they greet you with the colour, aroma and the elevated feeling the entrance exudes.

So, having the presence of the five elements of wood, fire, earth, water and metal at the entrance would run like this:

i.   Blue pots with

ii. Pink, red geraniums

iii. Either side of the door

iv. Terracotta saucers

v.   With a blue, green, red, black door

vi. Metal chime or wooden chime

vii. Framing the Door so your eyes have one Focus, one direction pulling and alluring you inside.

viii. The five elements create the balance that appeals to peoples' senses and intuition: Fire –flowers, Water – blue pots, Metal – Chime, Wood – plants or bushes, - Earth – terracotta dish. All these elements nourish each other and they in turn nourish the person living and entering the residence.

7 Days To Transform Your Life

Kitchen- Wealth is in your Health

The kitchen is one of those **Power Hubs**. The energy of the food in the kitchen creates the energy for the people of the house. What people eat reflects in their mood and within the walls of their home.

As an occupational therapist visiting over 2000 homes, I've met a whole array of humanity and how they manage their kitchens is interesting. Wealth lies in the kitchen because it is the energy we consume that determines how we feel, look and perceive. In our current society having money to take care of your health is a necessity. However, many people squander their money on items that do not generate the wealth of health. In other societies food and how it is cooked and presented is integral to feeling wealthy and healthy, and people glow and shine because of that.

When you feel good because of what you eat and your degree of exercise, that in turn aligns with your mental health. What does it feel like to be healthy? Does it mean having an environment that elevates and expands rather than imprisons? Or is it when we feel great and alive within ourselves no restrictions physically, mentally and spiritually?

How can we transform our environment so we are setting ourselves up for health and wellbeing? In this case, the environment of the kitchen can set us up to feel increasingly healthier.

This power hub of the kitchen has a vibration because the food stored there has a vibration and resonance too. Choosing wisely what is in the cupboards is a first indicator of the degree of responsibility you have chosen towards yourself and your family. What is around the kitchen gives messages to the children; a bowl of fruit has always been an indicator of health and wealth.

It also reflects the balance of the five elemental colours of black, green, red, yellow, orange and white.

If your dining table is free from clutter and you have food laid out on it you can double the image of health and wealth by having a mirror reflecting the food. The degree of clutter on tables affects the emotional balance within people. It disturbs the second brain, which is the gut. Emotions are integral to our eating patterns and what, where and how we eat can help how we digest that food and one way is to keep the area clear.

Historically, those with the food were considered the wealthy people. Pictures and images of wholesome food on your walls, portrayed perhaps in jars have a grounding effect – pulses, rice, seeds and legumes. This is reflected back to you that you have food. What you are inviting is an abundance of the **healthy** food into your life so that you are taking care of yourself. This is why rice has been used for centuries in ceremonies in China and India and the Far East because it is a symbol of abundance, wealth and good fortune. A bowl of rice to eat was symbolic of huge wealth.

A strong image of the kitchens is families coming together to eat and talk. Laughter and a wholesome buzz relates to the intestines and stomach region too. Pictures and images on the walls of people laughing, dancing subliminally connect with delight, ease and healthiness of spirit when around food. My extensive travels demonstrate most cultures have situations where they eat together. Morocco, India, Thailand, Mexico and many more. However, the increasing design of properties, urban areas and the pull towards larger inner cities has created another form of eating.

Eating on the go or on your own is when social isolation happens.

Illustrate your walls with symbols of people coming together to eat like some of the Renoir classics. Togetherness is sharing. Even those eating alone can create this image for drawing people in to that space and vibration. Sharing the great vibrational food with friends and strangers. Tables that have only one place mat and one chair reinforces the "oneness" of just you. Even if you are living alone as many people do now it does not have to emphasize emptiness or loneliness. A combination of the pictures and placement mats, bowl of fruit, teapot or coffee pot signifying more than one are suggesting a place for many people to meet.

I operated an Airbnb in my own home and, whilst travelling and met people from all over the world in the kitchen. Some we shared meals with and it certainly harmonized relations and extended networks and links. Therefore, setting up the kitchen harnesses a spirit and message of giving and receiving. A message of blessing and gratitude that you have food to eat and there is a permanent energy of plenty; this can be depicted in your kitchen environment through images, pictures and symbols. Wherever gratitude is displayed, more shows up.

Where a kitchen is located can influence feeding a lot more people than you anticipated. If your kitchen Is the first room people enter from the outside, often you will attract many people to your kitchen for food!! I know this happened to me and I found myself busy with the Airbnb folks and cooking for them when I was not particularly good!! However, it brought a wealth of company, resources and cash flow to my door.

7 Days To Transform Your Life

I have set up properties for people to rent and showrooms for people to buy properties. In the kitchen I created a feeling of homeliness and safety. Make your tablecloths gingham as there are squares and they conform to the earth qualities. People feel safe in boxes – as long as it isn't for too long!!

Think of Earth - qualities of hessian, clay pots, squares, terracotta colours that create a wholesome feeling. The chakras in our bodies associated with intestine and stomach are depicted in yellow and orange. These are the two colours associated with earth element and nurturing. These are the qualities to draw into this space because you are in the business of nurturing your own emotions. Colours of apricot and peach are good for stabilizing appetite. How you arrange your cupboards and food storage can assist you in your eating patterns. Foods that are healthier are more accessible whilst those that are not, reduce them in quantity and keep them out of eyesight or delete them altogether. The energy of those foods needs to be reduced and this is how you take control over your own environment by selecting what nurtures you healthily in your own kitchen! If you do not discipline your space it will control you and that includes being vigilant about what foods you allow into that space. Patterns dictate so the food that controls your mental and emotional state will affect the mood of your space especially the kitchen as well as the general harmony within the home.

The vibration of the food affects your moods, emotions, and digestion! The processed foods have no chi or alive spirit – they are dead and this is what people are eating and then they wonder why they feel depressed and dead!!

Keep visual pictures, emblems, and symbols of fresh food around you and illustrate the five elements of food through colour; yellow – earth; red – fire; green- wood, black – water; magnolia – metal. Go find fresh foods that display these colours, put them together and you have created the best chi and balance to your food.

The two elements that fight with each in the kitchen are water and fire.

Ensure your taps and sink have some space away from the oven. Keep these separate and symbolically put between them the element of earth – ceramic dish or yellow cloth. Earth absorbs water and it consumes the fire element.

The fire or heart of any kitchen will always be the oven/hob. This symbolizes the fire energy within your own body, which is required for metabolism and action. Ensure there are no missing hob points or anything out of order as that creates a broken no heat energy. To duplicate that fire dynamic energy place a small mirror behind the fire stove – even if it is an electric hob – it still has a red glow when turned on. Here then we are coding the kitchen to bring subconscious messages feeding back to you that you are healthy and therefore wealthy.

All water taps, sinks, and portals should not be leaking as that is your water energy which is associated with the flow of cash coming in and going out. Having seen this example so many times in my clients' homes and once in my own made me realize this is of paramount importance! A leaky faucet is water pouring away. So any leaks is tantamount to your money running away.

Above all, if there is one thing that can ensure a steady flow of health and wealth it would be gratitude and blessings for the food you have in your kitchen. If there is a symbol that can epitomize this sentiment it will always bring double the blessings for the inhabitants.

Bedroom
Health, once again is emphasized in this room. The energy here is paramount to how you sleep, rejuvenate, heal and enjoy yourself. It is also a very important Power Hub of your home because it influences the energy you exude which in turn impacts your feelings.

The mood here needs to be healing, relaxing and the elements can be earth, wood and fire. You want to feel safe, nurtured and secure in your bed-earth element. Fire element will influence the passion, dynamism and the romance of the love side of your life. Wood element will be illustrated in monitoring the growth in your life as in nature; you are growing and renewing your energies all the time. Having Images on the wall of nature and with affirmations of rejuvenation will assist your mental and emotional states of being.

If possible, reduce any of the **metal** energies in the bedroom, as this wakes up the mind and its function is to analyze. You do not want to be focusing whilst trying to sleep or rejuvenate yourself. The increase in insomnia, stress, and emotionally related diseases is so huge across the world and has doubled in the U.K. and people **wonder what is wrong with them?** What they fail to realize is the blue light from all the screens of the TV, monitors, digital clocks, technology of the iPhone, and Android phones are actually interfering with their brain waves. When your brain should be re-energizing itself through wave formation, it is being disrupted hence; you may not be able to get a good night's sleep with these devices in your room. Any sharp edges or multiple squares of mirrors that distort your image or concept of yourself, or sharp edges attacks you psychically. Furniture and designs that have circles and roundedness have a smoothing off effect and tend to flow.

Your habits cause your toxicity. Can you really afford to have these habits any longer? Repeatedly doing the same thing over and over and this particular habit, asleep in a sea of technical devices, causes massive disruption in the circuit of your brain and body. Accountability and responsibility mean disconnect before ownership of your imagination, creativity and independence is no longer yours! Place a traditional alarm clock next to your bed as the cell phones create huge disturbances with the **cells** of your body. You can consider alternatives that will make you fall asleep – playing music not via the phone but through non-cellular devices.

7 Days To Transform Your Life

As you wake up what is the first thing you see? Aspects of nature allow us to connect with something deeper within ourselves; photos, designs or pictures of nature. For example, it could be a sunrise awaiting the day. It could be words once again that configure a feeling, or affirmations for your life. You could have your Feng Shui Vision Board facing you first thing in the morning.

You are combining the most important elements, coding them into your space and environment, which in turn is feeding back to you messages to affect your life for the better! This in itself is assisting you to change the perceptions of what you see in the reality that you have created on the outside.

Besides the obvious of clearing out clutter, make sure you cleanse this room leaving the windows open to remove all negative thoughts or negative dream states. A bowl of salt in this room draws water to the bowl. After a week throw out the salt altogether.

The orientation of your bed makes a huge difference to the quality of your sleep. Ensure you do not have your feet pointing to the door of the bedroom. That is known to be the coffin position. Attach your bed to a strong wall behind you, otherwise it's like being a ship not anchored anywhere. Keep metal away from the bed structure and replace it with wood. When you are in the bedroom you want your mind to switch off. Do not have a window behind you, as this does not provide sufficient support psychologically. Be aware of anything towering over you such as a shelf, beam or a cupboard as this creates a sense of pressure down on you.

Bringing romance and passion into your bedroom space allows an expression for that aspect of your life. From the textures of the quilts to the colours of the accessories, make sure there is some space in there for concepts of love, passion and romance; colours of orange, red, cerise, and purple. Images of two, or an ornament with two figurines – one of my clients placed this in his bedroom and not long after met his wife.

Have pictures of growth in nature or something that creates a feeling of peace or of passion. Plants take out oxygen in the evening, so it would be advisable not to keep them in the bedroom whilst sleeping.

The balance of health and wealth in your life is in the ability to switch off and rest. If you over work the mental aspect, eventually it falls apart because failing to see the wealth in rest and sleep has consequences. Have a reminder of a timer to go to bed at a certain time; have a ritual of writing down your results or achievements for the day-listing what you are grateful for so that these sentiments merge into your sub consciousness in preparation for the following day.

Finally, YOU!

Yes, you are the hub of the home and what energy you deliver into it will determine the quality of the time spent there.

The real hub is what is going on between your two ears and the four walls – the most expensive real estate in the world. We are talking about transforming our environments but part of that change has to come from you! The internal architecture. The energy exuded by you is pouring into your space. Revolutionary results call for revolutionary changes within you. It is the only revolution worth fighting for because what comes from that is the changes created in your life, which ripple to your own environment and your own community, ultimately the world.

When I first arrived at a particular street twenty-five years ago it was very dour. I started placing hanging baskets outside, pots with flowers on either side of the door. I changed the colour of the door, and above it placed blue bottles for light to shine through. Years later I returned to the property, which is now rented, the tenant understood Feng Shui and continued with similar ideas. Lo and behold all the residents have flowers in their pots, hanging baskets, and chimes hanging in their entrances. The local government has planted trees along the walkway making a big difference to the energy. The whole street now celebrates an annual party where they come together from diverse backgrounds. That is success!

This is about investing in the energy of you.

Success is you accepting and making the most of you. Not what others sublimely tell you is success or what has been piped into the education, media outlets pervading our very own consciousness so that we have no idea who we are but we hand over our power to some celebrity who represents NOTHING.

Only you can invest in yourself and one way to get started is to promote the change you wish to represent, you wish to draw towards you by surrounding yourself with it. Through your own creativity you can place the colours, aromas, feelings, geometry, sounds, pictures, and shapes in the space you reside. What you have around you is symbolic of what it is you want to create within you, whether that is love, passion, peace, Zen, health, wealth, philanthropy, business, family, and rest.

You have to invest the energies that you hold within you whether that is a new healthy eating pattern, an exercise discipline, a new challenge or creating a better habit with fitness, food or finances.

The pain of not investing in yourself energetically emerges many years later as your emotional, financial and spiritual landscape lies bankrupt. Taking action by doing these 7 Days outlined in this book will lay the foundations for transformation in the years to come. If you don't prepare or take control over the environment in which you live, then how are you expected to recognize the opportunities when they come towards you?

You will have aligned your own inner energies alongside the code you have created on the outside so that the chances of some of that happening and being fruitful far outweigh doing absolutely nothing or wishing for the best and blindly being led where the bigger authorities want control.

ACTION & EXERCISES

ENTRANCE

• Change colour of door

• Put some blue pots and pink/red flowers on either side of door

• Ensure the brasses, letterbox, and bell are working and shining

• Ensure all five elements are present

• Ensure you have some aromatic herbs by the door to smell as you come in and out

• Take away all clutter from the front entrance

KITCHEN

- Choose pictures that support your abundance and warmth you want to be surrounded by in your kitchen.

- Put a mirror up on wall where you serve and eat so it is duplicating food, which is health and wealth.

- Managing mind issues regarding food and where it is located; putting forbidden foods away in the cupboard of your mind is mirrored in your kitchen. Have foods that are healthy more accessible and unhealthy foods, whether biscuits or cakes, out of reach. Better still, take those foods from the kitchen altogether, change behavior and don't bring them in.

- On your fridge, or walls have a message either in words, pictures or symbols that reflect back to you what being healthy is for you! Words impact our minds and having to repeat them sublimely each time you are in the kitchen – creates a normalizing response to align your goals around what is healthy.

BEDROOM

- Mirrors, especially facing you whilst sleeping or at the sidewall where the bed is positioned, are considered radiators of movement. They duplicate images in the night therefore does not make for a good night's sleep nor symbolically signify healing.

- What kind of peace or message is your bedroom reflecting back to you? Are the pictures peaceful or is the energy full of clutter. What habit have you created in here that keeps being repeated but is detrimental to your health and quality of sleep?

- The bedroom is a place to restore your cells, to relax and rest, for peace and rejuvenation.

- If you are looking to attract someone special, then have a symbol of two in this place – no single images – colours of pink, rose quartz, and red.

- What is the feeling and the picture you wake up to first thing in the morning as that has a huge impact on your subconscious. Place a picture of the sun rising, or images of nature with powerhouse mottos.

- The colours to have around you would be for healing and resting – green, pale blue, pinks, yellow.

YOU!

- Be aware of what energies you hold in yourself and how they have a bearing on the spaces in which you live, work and walk daily.

- Transforming your life is about transforming you. Try wearing different coloured clothes – go through the vibrant reds, maroons to the greens, and finishing with the lilacs and whites. Make a note of any comments or responses people may make whilst wearing these colours.

- Go to work on a different route and write down what is it you are noticing.

- Go to different places to shop and notice what these environments bring out in you as a person.

- Try eating no white sugar for two weeks and notice your moods, emotions and behavior. These are the kinds of changes that will warrant comment from yourself and others.

- If you drink alcohol; do not drink for two weeks and notice how people change around you, the attitudes and what it brings out in you.

- Do one thing each week that takes you out of your comfort zone and watch how your personality responds.

- **For those who would still like to have assistance in this matter you can contact me for Skype calls or consultations: www.wealthyspaces.com**

CONCLUSION

These 7 days have been about setting the foundations, sowing the seeds for you to be the architect of your own Life and Destiny. By the end of this book I would say you are paying more attention to your surroundings and how it is affecting you. You are feeling lighter within yourself and the environment is reflecting back more space to go forward in your life. The flow of your energy is going in the direction of your own vision board.

That expression if only walls could talk begins to make some kind of sense. The walls of where you live, work and spend most time are talking to you all the time. You need to make sure they are telling you what you need to hear instead of some other person's story.

The intention of this book was to assist people in their daily life by taking some simple active steps to clear away their weapons of mass distraction. When you have electronic devices to monitors and messages of the marketing world vying for your attention daily, where is your own voice and sense of peace?

These 7 days can be started anytime but NOW is always the best time.

7 Days To Transform Your Life

I have tried to awaken the space where you reside and invited you to create a message, a reflection that supports you in your life. It can help with eating issues, dealing with mental health issues, and wellbeing in terms of clarity, decisiveness, and reducing the levels of self-sabotage. The main aim is to change the frequency, vibration and resonance of yourself through your space so that you become the King or Queen of your own Kingdom. You have control over the kaleidoscope of meanings you want to perceive when you take control over your own space.

On a philosophical note, there are no beginnings or ends in the cycle of the elements, in the processes of your life. The space is YOU, YOU are the space. It is all YOU!

From Day 1 to Day 7 what seeds you sow will have an exponentially compounding effect on your life. By now you begin to realize that having self mastery of your home and business environments start to alter the perceptions of how you see your own world and where and what it is you want in it. Your perceptions will change, your repeated messages, direction and internal feelings will start to calibrate with what you really want to show up in your life on the outside.

If you take anything away it is to wake you up and realize that the environment is the habit that you have established for yourself most of the time it is unconscious. When you start tackling the visible obstacles and invisible blocks you notice truly what has always been there for you; opportunities, abundance, going beyond self-sabotage, and inviting self-compassion. Most importantly, all these distractions around us that stop us from our clarity, focus will be obvious and it will be our choice to focus on our Feng Shui Vision Board rather than the T.V.! Remember to always make room for Magik in your space. If you have no space how can your life shift into places and areas you want to attract?

The 7 Days can be modified to 7 weeks for those with time constraints or large properties or the nature of the clutter is well and truly entrenched. It is still possible to conduct a week of decluttering, a week of space cleansing and so on.

As a result of taking ACTION on these seven days/weeks I know you will feel a huge difference to your life energetically and perceptually.

"BE STILL AND KNOW"

7 Days To Transform Your Life

Links for all Meditation, Visualisations, Tapping Videos, Youtube Videos

https://www.wealthyspaces.com - resources

Clutter List

Tapping Videos - http://bit.ly/2B7q71k

Youtube Channel - http://bit.ly/2KjRiIt

Meditation Video – http://bit.ly/2ToaKZK

Decluttering Interview – http://bit.ly/2MDcITI

Shapes & Colour Book - http://bit.ly/2BnatQ8

Mandala Designs - https://inspiredtoinspire.co.uk/

Contact Details http://wealthyspaces.com/product/package-1/

FACEBOOK   https://www.facebook.com/wealthyspaces/

LINKEDIN   https://www.linkedin.com/in/healthyspaces/

INSTAGRAM   https://www.instagram.com/FENGSHUI4YOU/

TWITTER   https://twitter.com/cathi888